What Every Advisor Needs to Know About Trusts

Save Taxes, Protect Assets & Preserve Wealth

Roger D. Silk, Ph.D.

Katherine A. Silk, M.A.

For information about this title or to order other books and/or
electronic media, contact the publisher:

Sterling Lifetime Press
www.sterlingfoundations.com

ISBNs:
Hardcover ISBN: 978-1-968778-02-6
Paperback ISBN
eBook ISBN

10 9 8 7 6 5 4 3 2 1

Printed in the United States of America

Disclaimer

This publication is intended solely for educational and informational purposes. It is not intended to provide, and shall not be construed as providing, legal, tax, accounting, financial, or other professional advice. The application and impact of laws can vary widely based on the specific facts and circumstances involved. Therefore, readers are strongly encouraged to consult with qualified legal, tax, and financial professionals prior to making any decisions based on the content of this book.

The author, the author's employer, all affiliated and related entities, and the publisher expressly disclaim any and all liability for any direct, indirect, incidental, consequential, punitive, or other damages whatsoever arising out of or relating to the use of, reference to, or reliance on the information presented in this book. This includes, without limitation, any errors or omissions in the content, or any outcomes resulting from the use of any strategies, structures, or interpretations discussed herein.

No representations or warranties, express or implied, are made as to the accuracy, completeness, reliability, or timeliness of the information contained in this book. The material is provided "as is," with no guarantee of fitness for a particular purpose or outcome.

The mention of any specific strategy, entity, structure, product, or service does not constitute an endorsement or recommendation by the author, the author's employer, their affiliates, or the publisher. Examples, case studies, and hypothetical scenarios provided herein are for illustrative purposes only and do not represent or imply any guarantee of results, and should not be interpreted as literal reports of actual cases. Any resemblance of names and situations to real people is entirely coincidental.

Laws, regulations, and professional standards are subject to change. Nothing in this book should be interpreted as a guarantee or warranty of any sort that any particular tax or legal treatment will be sustained under examination or litigation.

Contents

1. Introduction

If you advise high net worth investors and you have not studied the field of trusts, you are likely to find considerable value in gaining an increased understanding and appreciation of trusts, and what they can do for high net worth families.

The purpose of this book is to provide readers with enough knowledge to be informed about the uses of trusts and some of the problems trusts can solve.

Neither this book, nor any single book, will make you an expert. But you don't have to be an expert in trusts to benefit from using them, any more than you have to be an expert airplane mechanic to travel by air.

Key Problems that Trusts Can Solve

If you need to drive a nail, a hammer is usually the best tool. But if you need to drive a screw, you'll be much better off with a screwdriver.

To accomplish goals efficiently and effectively, it's usually best to use the right tool. And unless the problems are very simple, it's usually best to have the tool in the hands of an expert.

This book discusses a wide range of problems for which trust tools and solutions have been developed. Among the main categories of problems for which trust tools exist are:

- **Taxes**: Reducing, Avoiding, and Deferring
- **Asset Protection**: Protecting Assets from Potential Creditors
- **Control**: Managing and Controlling Cash Flows
- **Access**: Managing and Controlling Access to Cash and Assets
- **Legacy**: Providing for Current and Future Generations

Focus On US Context

The concept of a trust as we know it in the United States originated in England, perhaps as long as a thousand years ago. The law of trusts is largely restricted to the English-speaking world, and places where the influence of the English common law was and is strong. In Louisiana, a state whose legal system is originates in the Napoleonic Code, trusts were not recognized until the state enacted legislation specifically recognizing trusts. Quebec in Canada has done something similar. In most of the world, trusts remain a relatively foreign concept.

But if you're reading this, chances are good that you live in a country that recognizes trusts, or that you're a US citizen. If you're a US citizen, regardless of where you live you need to concern yourself with the effect of US laws on family wealth.

Trusts have been used by wealthy families for centuries. But since the introduction of the income tax and the estate tax in the United States in 1916, trusts have become increasingly important vehicles for the preservation and growth of wealth.

This book is aimed at Americans, and the great majority of the material concerns US laws, and the use of trusts in a US context.

A Note on the Use of Acronyms and Initialisms

In many discussions of trusts, you can feel like you fell into a bowl of alphabet soup. It is common to read or hear people using strange "words" like *ilit* or *SNT*. These are usually either *acronyms* or *initialisms*.

An acronym is a word formed from the first letters of a multi-word term. For example, the "word" ILIT (pronounced "eye-lit" is formed from the first letters of the term "irrevocable life insurance trust."

An initialism is similar to an acronym, but each letter is usually pronounced. For example, *United States* is frequently represented by the initialism *US*, and each letter is pronounced.

Many people upon hearing or reading a new (to them) acronym or initialism will forget what it means. For that reason, in this book, we have tried to reduce the use of both, and instead spell out the full term as much as possible. However, we have included many common acronyms and initialisms so that if you run into them elsewhere, you will be able to look up what they mean.

At the end of this book, we have included a glossary of some of the more common acronyms and initialisms. If you're reading and run into one, that's a good place to check.

WHAT'S NEXT

When thoughtfully selected and skillfully implemented, the right trust structure can be a highly effective solution to a wide range of financial, tax, and legacy planning challenges. While many of the trusts described in this book may at first seem complex or unfamiliar, and indeed many of them are, each exists to solve a specific set of problems that affluent families face.

The book begins with a short review of the origins of trusts, and an even shorter summary of the key elements of a trust.

The remainder of the chapters are divided into six sections, namely:

- Basics and Basic Taxation
- Advanced Tax Planning Trusts
- Charitable Trusts and Special Rules
- Estate Planning and Family Trusts
- Asset Protection Trusts
- Special Purpose Trusts

2. Origins

ORIGINS IN MEDIEVAL ENGLAND

The Trust law that we have in the US today traces its origins all the way back to the early Middle Ages. The development of the institution of a Trust may have been sparked by the Crusades. During the 12th and 13th centuries, English knights and nobles would embark on long, hazardous journeys to the Holy Land, leaving their estates and properties behind.

To manage their assets in their absence, they transferred the legal title of their properties to trusted individuals, known as "trustees," who would manage the properties for the benefit of the knights' families. This arrangement relied on trust (in the everyday meaning of the term: "assured reliance on the character, ability, strength, or truth of someone or something" as Merriam Webster defines it) and was the precursor to the modern legal institution of trusts.

THE COURT OF CHANCERY AND EQUITY

The early common law did not recognize trusts. The development of trust law was significantly influenced by the establishment of the Court of Chancery in the 14th century. The Court of Chancery, presided over by the Lord Chancellor, recognized and enforced trusts, even though trusts were not acknowledged by common law courts.

STATUTE OF USES

The evolution of trust law took a significant turn with the enactment of the Statute of Uses in the year 1535. Before the statute, one person could allow another person to use his land, but the land-owner still had to pay taxes on it. Under the Statute, if a person transferred land to another person to use, the user would be considered the owner for tax purposes. People began using trusts to circumvent this outcome.

The Statute of Uses is considered by many to have laid the groundwork for the separation of legal and equitable titles, a fundamental aspect of modern trust law.

MODERN TRUST LAW

By the 19th century, trust law had matured significantly. The Trustee Act of 1850 and the Trustee Act of 1925 codified principles and rules governing the administration of trusts. These acts clarified the duties and powers of trustees, established guidelines for the investment of trust property, and provided mechanisms for the appointment and removal of trustees. The flexibility and adaptability of trust law allowed it to be used in various contexts, such as family settlements, charitable trusts, and pension funds. But we move across the Atlantic to see the fullest flowering of trust law.

COLONIAL PERIOD AND EARLY DEVELOPMENT

The colonization of America by English settlers brought with it the English legal system, including the legal principles of equity[1] and trust law. However, the application and evolution of trust law in the United States were shaped by the unique social, economic, and political conditions of the developing nation.

In the colonial period, trusts were primarily used for family settlements and the management of estates. The influence of English trust law was evident, but the American legal system began to develop its own distinct characteristics.

The adoption of written constitutions and the establishment of state legislatures allowed for the adaptation and modification of English legal principles to suit American needs.

---

[1] https://www.law.cornell.edu/wex/equity states: "In law, the term "equity" refers to a particular set of remedies and associated procedures involved with civil law. These equitable doctrines and procedures are distinguished from "legal" ones. While legal remedies typically involve monetary damages, equitable relief typically refers to injunction, specific performance, or vacatur. A court will usually award equitable remedies when a legal remedy is insufficient or inadequate. For example, courts will generally award equitable relief for a claim which involves a particular or unique piece of real estate, or if the plaintiff requests specific performance."

THE RISE OF CHARITABLE TRUSTS

For reasons that are not fully understood, but are part cultural, part historical, part legislative, Americans are the most charitable people in the world.

Thus, it is perhaps not surprising that a significant development in American trust law was the rise of charitable trusts. In the 19th century, the growth of philanthropic activities and the establishment of charitable institutions led to an increased use of trusts for charitable purposes. A Massachusetts court, in Jackson v. Phillips, in 1867, gave a definition often attributed to be that of a charitable trust:

A charity in the legal sense may be more fully defined as a gift, to be applied consistently with existing laws, for the benefit of an indefinite number of persons, either by bringing their minds or hearts under the influence of education or religion, by relieving their bodies from disease, suffering or constraint, by assisting them to establish themselves in life, or by creating and maintaining public buildings or works, or otherwise lessening the burdens of government.

THE RESTATEMENT (SECOND) OF TRUSTS AND THE UNIFORM TRUST CODE

In the 20th century, efforts were made to standardize and modernize trust law across the United States. The Restatement (Second) of Trusts, published by the American Law Institute in 1959, provided a comprehensive summary of the principles of trust law and served as a guide for judges and practitioners.

Another significant development was the creation of the Uniform Trust Code (UTC) in 2000. The UTC aimed to provide a uniform set of rules and guidelines for the creation, administration, and termination of trusts. It addressed issues such as the duties and powers of trustees, the rights of beneficiaries, and the modification and termination of trusts. The adoption of the UTC by many states helped to harmonize trust law across the country and provided greater clarity and predictability for trust administration.

TRUSTS IN MODERN AMERICA

Today, trusts are widely used in the United States for a variety of purposes, including estate planning, asset protection, care of people unable to take care of themselves (e.g. special needs), and charitable giving. The flexibility and versatility of trusts make them valuable tools for managing, growing and preserving wealth. The development of specialized trusts, such as revocable living trusts, grantor and non-grantor irrevocable trusts, and spendthrift trusts, allows individuals to tailor their plans (including providing for people, minimizing taxes, asset protection, care of people, provide for charity etc.) to meet their specific needs and objectives.

While trust law in England and the United States shares common roots, there are notable differences in their development and application. English trust law has remained closely tied to its origins, with a strong emphasis on the fiduciary duties of trustees. In contrast, American trust law has evolved to address the diverse needs of a dynamic and heterogeneous society, incorporating principles from both common law and statutory frameworks.

STATE OF CHOICE

Though it is a matter of opinion and there is no universal agreement, Delaware has traditionally been considered a very favorable state for establishing a trust in the U.S. due to its robust legal framework, favorable tax treatment, and strong asset protection laws. Delaware allows for perpetual trusts, meaning trusts can last indefinitely without being subject to the Rule Against Perpetuities.[2] It also offers significant privacy for trust beneficiaries and grantors, with minimal disclosure requirements. Additionally, Delaware's tax laws do not impose state income tax on trusts created by non-residents, making it a tax-efficient choice. Other states that are considered in the same category include Nevada, South Dakota, and last but not least, Alaska.

WHAT IS REQUIRED TO ESTABLISH A TRUST?

The minimum requirements for a trust generally include the following elements:

Trustor/Settlor/Grantor: The person who creates the trust.

Trustee: The person or entity that manages the trust assets according to the trust agreement. (In some instances, this can be the grantor.)

---

[2] The rule against perpetuities is a principle that holds that a trust cannot last more than 21 years after the death of a life-in-being (life in existence) at the creation of the trust.

Beneficiary: The person or entity that benefits from the trust. In some cases, this can be the grantor, in which case the trust is "self-settled."

Trust Property: The assets or property placed into the trust.

Intent: The clear intention to create a trust, typically expressed in the trust document. Typically, the trust document will include an expression of intent.

Valid Trust Purpose: The trust must have a lawful purpose and not violate public policy.

Clear Expression: This almost always means a written trust document, properly evidenced by the laws of the governing state.

3. Revocable Trusts for Non-Taxable Estates

EARLY TRUST CONCEPTS AND THE BIRTH OF THE REVOCABLE LIVING TRUST

As we discussed in the previous chapter, the modern legal entity that we call a "Trust" dates back to medieval England, but the specific idea of the revocable trust (also called a "living trust") developed in America.

We can't say "United States" because it is believed that the first revocable trust was established in 1765 for Francis Fauquier, who was the Lieutenant Governor of Virginia, and for whom Fauquier County in Virginia is named. There was no country called the United States of America until September 9, 1776. (Yes, apparently, we all learned it wrong. The Constitution Center has a fuller explanation.[3])

As you will recall, a trust is a legal arrangement in which one person (natural or corporate) legally owns and manages property for the benefit of another party. The person who owns and manages the property is called the trustee, and the person on whose behalf the property is being managed is the beneficiary.

Revocable trusts can be designed to achieve various objectives, including managing assets, avoiding probate, providing for future generations, and as standby beneficiaries for avoiding the SECURE act tax on retirement plans.

As the word revocable implies, a revocable trust is characterized by its flexibility: the person who creates the trust (typically called the grantor or settlor) retains the right to change the terms, or completely cancel (i.e. revoke) the trust during that person's lifetime. This right distinguishes it from irrevocable trusts, which cannot be changed once they are established.

---

[3] https://constitutioncenter.org/blog/today-the-name-united-states-of-america-becomes-offici

EVOLUTION IN THE MID-20TH CENTURY

The revocable or living trust gained popularity in the mid-20th century as an estate planning tool. There are (at least) three major factors that have driven the popularity of living trusts.

Probate

One of the primary motivations for using a revocable living trust is to avoid probate. Probate is the legal process through which a deceased person's estate is settled and distributed. It can be time-consuming, expensive, and public, as well as subject to dispute by heirs and would-be heirs.

By owning assets in a revocable living trust, individuals can ensure that their assets are transferred to beneficiaries without the need for probate,[4] thereby saving time and money and maintaining privacy.

When the grantor dies, the trust becomes irrevocable. Thus, the rules for who gets what, when, become "written in stone" as it were, and the grantor's wishes should be respected.

Incapacity Planning

A second potential benefit of a living trust is to provide a mechanism for managing assets in the event the grantor becomes incapacitated. If the grantor, (we'll call him Adam), is no longer able to manage his own affairs, a co-trustee or successor trustee can smoothly step in and manage the trust assets on Adam's behalf, without the need for delays, cost or uncertainty involved in a court proceeding.

Flexibility and Control

A third benefit of the revocability of the trust is that it provides the grantor with the ability to change his (or her) mind. A revocable trust can easily be amended, meaning that the grantor retains full control over his or her assets and makes changes as his or her circumstances or wishes change. This flexibility makes the revocable living trust an attractive option for many people.

---

[4] Trusts avoid probate because the probate process applies to the property in the decedent's estate. But the property owned by the trust is not, in general, in the decedent's estate for probate purposes.

COMMON USES FOR NON-TAXABLE ESTATES

In recent decades, the use of revocable living trusts has continued to grow, particularly for non-taxable estates. A non-taxable estate is one that falls below the federal estate tax exemption threshold, meaning it is not subject to federal estate taxes. As of 2024, the federal estate tax exemption is approximately $13.6 million per individual, meaning most estates in the United States are not subject to federal estate tax.

For non-taxable estates, the primary benefits of a revocable living trust are probate avoidance and incapacity planning, rather than tax planning. However, the living trust offers several other advantages that make it a valuable tool for estate planning:

PRIVACY

Unlike a will, which becomes a public document upon probate, a revocable living trust remains private. This means the details of the estate, including the assets and the identities of the beneficiaries, are not made public. For many families, this privacy alone justifies the use of a living trust to own most of the family's assets.

EFFICIENCY IN ASSET DISTRIBUTION

Probate can be a slow, cumbersome and expensive process. A living trust can bypass that process. Assets held in a living trust can be distributed to beneficiaries more quickly than assets that must go through probate. This can enable the estate executor (who might also be the trustee) to close the estate faster and with less hassle and expense than if probate had to be concluded.

REDUCED COSTS

As noted, avoiding probate should also avoid most of the costs associated with probate court fees, attorney fees, and other administrative expenses connected to probate. This can result in significant savings for the estate.

SIMPLIFICATION OF MULTI-STATE PROPERTY OWNERSHIP

What's worse than going through probate? Going through probate in multiple states.

Some people who own property in multiple states, or rather, their heirs, may discover the hard way that they are responsible for going through probate in each state in which they own property. This requirement can be avoided if the properties are owned in a revocable trust. During the owner's lifetime, the owner retains all the control and flexibility. Only when the owner dies does the trust become irrevocable. For individuals who own property in multiple states, a revocable living trust can simplify the transfer of those properties by avoiding multiple probate proceedings in different states.

LEGAL FRAMEWORK AND REGULATION

The legal framework for revocable living trusts is primarily governed by state law, and there are some variations from state to state. However, most states have adopted provisions of the Uniform Trust Code (UTC), which provides a comprehensive set of rules for the creation, administration, and termination of trusts. The UTC aims to standardize trust law across states, providing greater clarity and consistency.

Some of the key states that have not adopted the UTC include Delaware, Nevada, Alaska and South Dakota, all considered good jurisdictions in which to domicile a trust. These states have not adopted the UTC because they believe (and many trust grantors and attorneys agree) that their own state laws are better for trust grantors and beneficiaries than the UTC rules.

TRUSTEE DUTIES

A trustee has a fiduciary duty to act in the best interests of the beneficiaries of the trust. This duty encompasses several key responsibilities, including:

Duty of Loyalty: The trustee must prioritize the interests of the beneficiaries above their own and avoid conflicts of interest.

Duty of Care: The trustee must manage the trust assets prudently, making informed decisions and seeking expert advice when necessary. State law permitting, a trustee may delegate investment responsibility to an investment manager who is not the trustee.

Duty of Impartiality: The trustee must treat all beneficiaries fairly and impartially, considering their respective interests.

Trustees are legally and ethically bound to uphold these duties, ensuring the trust's purpose is fulfilled and the beneficiaries' rights are protected.

ESTABLISHING A TRUST

Establishment of a revocable trust involves several steps. Among these are:

Drafting

The trust document, or trust agreement, outlines the terms and conditions of the trust, including the identification of the grantor, trustee, and beneficiaries, as well as the distribution plan for the trust assets. Technically, a trust does not have to be drafted by a lawyer. However, in almost every circumstance it will be prudent to have the advice of someone who has knowledge and experience relevant to the situation of the grantor, so that the terms of the trust can accurately reflect the grantor's desires and situation.

Funding

A trust doesn't technically exist until it owns something. Thus, assets must be transferred into the trust, even if only $10.

In the old days, it was reportedly common for trust lawyers to have drawers full of trust documents that had a dollar, or a ten-dollar bill, stapled to them, representing that the trust had been funded.

For most modern purposes, the assets that the grantor wants in the trust need to be titled to the trust by some process. This involves changing the title of the assets to the name of the trust. Common assets placed in a revocable living trust include real estate, bank accounts, investments, and personal property.

Management and Administration

During the grantor's lifetime, the grantor may, and typically does, serve as the trustee. The grantor may continue to manage the trust assets, though it is also common to have a professional manage the trust's investment. Upon the grantor's incapacity or death, the successor trustee takes over the management and distribution of the trust assets according to the terms of the trust document.

PRACTICAL CONSIDERATIONS

While the benefits of revocable living trusts are clear, there are also practical considerations. Among these are:

Initial Setup and Titling

Achieving a grantor's objectives using a living trust requires careful thought and planning. The grantor has to think about and make decisions that some people would rather postpone. Among such decisions are who will get what, when, either while the grantor lives or more frequently after the grantor's death. Effectively translating those desires into enforceable language will usually require legal assistance, which can involve initial setup costs.

Once the trust is set up, the next step is to transfer the assets into the trust. That process can be a bit of a pain, requiring paperwork, and often back and forth with several representatives of whatever custodian holds the assets. But once done, it should not have to be redone.

Potential Complexity

For some individuals, the additional complexity of managing a trust may be off putting. However, working with experienced legal and financial professionals can help navigate this complexity.

Common Misconceptions

There are common misconceptions about revocable living trusts, such as the belief that they provide asset protection from creditors, or somehow make the assets and income less subject to tax. In the vast majority of cases, neither of those is true. Because the grantor retains control over the trust assets, revocable trusts typically do not offer the same level of asset protection as irrevocable trusts. And because, by definition, all revocable trusts are grantor trusts, revocable trusts have essentially no effect on income taxes.

4. Grantor Trusts: What Good Are They?

In this chapter, we discuss what grantor trusts are, their most common uses, and how they can be used to help people avoid or minimize estate and gift taxes.

For most purposes, the key feature of a grantor trust (as opposed to any of several varieties of non-grantor trust) is the fact that the income earned by a grantor trust flows through to the grantor's personal income tax return.

Why would someone want to pay tax on income that doesn't flow to him or her?

That is the question we'll address in this chapter.

As it turns out, counter-intuitive though it may appear at first, having to pay tax on the income generated by a trust can be an advantage in estate planning.

To repeat, the key characteristic of a grantor trust is that, for federal income tax purposes, the trust's income is taxed to the grantor, not to the trust itself or the beneficiaries (unless a grantor is also a beneficiary, in which case the income will be taxed to the grantor in the grantor's role as grantor, not the grantor's role as beneficiary). This differs from a non-grantor trust, in which case the trust itself or its beneficiaries are responsible for taxes on the trust's income.

COMMON TYPES OF GRANTOR TRUSTS

Several types of grantor trusts are commonly used, each with its own specific purposes and benefits:

Revocable or Living Trust: A revocable trust is a grantor trust. That is, any revocable trust will, by its nature, pass any income earned or recognized by the trust to the grantor for federal income tax purposes. Living trusts are typically used for non-tax reasons, and the grantor nature of the trust has no tax-planning significance.

Irrevocable Life Insurance Trust (ILIT): A trust designed to own life insurance policies, typically also designed to make sure that the death benefits are out of the grantor's estate for estate tax purposes, is often called an ILIT. One design calls for the trust to be a grantor trust, and during the grantor's life it has little income and the grantor design has limited income tax effects.

Grantor Retained Annuity Trust (GRAT): A GRAT is a type of trust specifically designed with estate planning purposes in mind. A full discussion of GRATs is beyond the scope of this book. We plan a future book to discuss GRATs in greater depth.

Intentionally [Defective] Grantor Trust: A trust may be designed as a grantor trust that takes assets out of the grantor's estate for estate tax purposes, but leaves the income with the grantor for income tax purposes.[5]

In the early days of grantor trusts, some lawyers inadvertently drafted trusts that were considered grantor trusts, and this may be the origin of the term "defective." The term has stuck, and is still sometimes used. You may often see the term Intentionally Defective Grantor trust, or simply Grantor trust.

INCOME TAXES

In some circumstances, a grantor trust can be used to shift the income tax burden from the trust or its beneficiaries to the grantor. This can be advantageous if, for example, the beneficiaries might be in a higher tax bracket than the grantor, or if the grantor desires to pay the income tax instead of having either the trust or the beneficiaries pay the income tax.

Trust Income Tax

If a trust is not a grantor trust, and it has only taxable beneficiaries, the trust is likely to be a complex trust. A complex trust is a taxable trust. Such trusts, as opposed to individuals, pay tax at the highest personal income tax bracket on the income over $14,450 (as of this writing).

Thus, in most cases, a taxable trust will pay a higher total income tax on a given amount of income compared to the total amount of income tax that would be paid if the

---

[5] Prior to the 1940s, there was no such thing as a grantor trust. The supreme court, in a decision designed to increase tax revenue, ruled (Helvering v. Clifford, 1940), created the concept of a trust whose income was taxable to the grantor. Congress codified the grantor trust in 1954.

same amount of income were spread over one or more human beneficiaries.

In many estate planning situations, the desire is not to pay more income tax than necessary. So, either the beneficiaries or the grantor, rather than the trust, should pay the tax, because they'll be taxed at a lower rate than the trust would.

Why Have the Grantor Pay Income Tax on Trust Income?

If a trust is not itself to be liable for tax, then either the grantor or the beneficiaries will have to be liable.

In estate planning situations, it is often the case that the grantor is trying to remove as much value from his estate as possible, while incurring as little estate or gift tax as possible.

A grantor trust can be a way to effectively carry this out.

Consider a case in which a grantor funds a non-grantor trust with property worth exactly the amount of his remaining lifetime estate/gift tax exemption. For ease of illustration, let's assume this amount is $10,000,000.

Again, for ease of illustration, assume the trust invests and earns exactly 5.1445% interest per year, or $514,450 of ordinary income.

At trust tax rates, the trust will owe tax at the top ordinary income tax rate, 37%, on $500,000 of income.

Compare that to a couple filing jointly in 2024, which would incur the top rate of 37% only on income above $731,000, and would pay 35% only on income above $487,000.

If the $514,450 were the couple's only taxable income, they'd owe about $113,000 in income tax on it (assuming no state or other income taxes).

That same income, in the trust, would incur taxes of over $185,000.

The difference in this example is over $70,000, and would occur each year.

Extra Gift

Another reason for using a grantor trust, as opposed to a non-grantor (complex) trust, is to increase the effective gift.

Using the same numbers as above, if the non-grantor trust must pay tax (as opposed to the grantor absorbing the tax), the trust will have $185,000 less after the year.

So, in effect, the grantor makes an additional "gift" of $185,000 to the trust by making the trust a grantor trust. That extra $185,000 is not considered a taxable gift.

And it can be argued that the grantor provision is worth even more than that $185,000 a year. Suppose that the grantor was to have the trust pay the $185,000 of income taxes, and then the grantor would make an additional gift to make up for the $185,000 paid in taxes.

That would cost the grantor about $259,000, because the gift itself would be taxable. If the grantor has no remaining gift/estate tax exemption, to make a gift of $185,000, the giver would also have to pay a gift tax of $74,000.

Sale of Assets to an Intentionally Defective Grantor Trust

A grantor trust can be used as a buyer of appreciated assets that a grantor believes will keep appreciating. The sale of such assets to a grantor trust can remove the asset from the estate for estate tax purposes, while avoiding the recognition of capital gain.

For example, the grantor can sell appreciating assets to the grantor trust in exchange for a promissory note. The sale is not recognized for income tax purposes, and any future appreciation of the assets occurs outside the grantor's estate, reducing future estate taxes.

The note will have to bear interest, and that interest will come back into the grantor's estate for tax purposes.

Sale of Appreciated Assets and Avoidance of Capital Gains Tax

Consider a grantor with no remaining estate tax exemption, but with remaining appreciated assets in his estate. He wants to get the assets out of his estate but doesn't want to incur either capital gains taxes, or estate/gift taxes.

One strategy is to use first a tax-exempt Asset Diversification Trust, and then an Intentionally Defective Grantor Trust.

The asset would be contributed to the Asset Diversification Trust. Because the Asset Diversification Trust is tax-exempt, that trust can sell the asset, and incur no capital gains tax.

The grantor owns the lead interest in the Asset Diversification Trust. The grantor then sells that lead interest to the grantor trust, for a note.

5. Tax Drag in Investing

Tax drag—the reduction of an investment's returns due to taxation—is a hidden but damaging force. Left unchecked, tax drag will erode and destroy wealth over time, as certainly as water running downhill over soil will dig out channels, wash away dirt, and eventually turn whole mountains into plains.

Morningstar has estimated that tax drag costs the average investor about 1.8% per year![6]

For investors and their financial advisors, understanding and addressing tax drag is a highly leveraged way to deliver low-risk, significant long-term value to high net worth investors. This guide explores what tax drag is, how it arises, and includes strategies investors (or their advisors) can implement to help preserve more of their hard-earned portfolios' growth.

Tax Drag

Taxes reduce returns not only in the short term but also impede the compounding process that is essential for building wealth. Consider a portfolio with a gross return of 8% annually and a 30% effective tax rate. The after-tax return shrinks to just 5.6%.

Over a single year, this shrinkage might seem minor. But the cost --when compounded over an investing lifetime, or a working lifetime -- can be huge.

An example of this cost is below.

Consider an initial investment of $10,000. After one year, at 8%, the investment grows to $10,800. After tax at 30% on the growth, the ending investment value is $10,560. The difference is material, but not huge.

However, consider the average investor who has a 40-year time horizon (e.g. age 40 to age 80, age 50 to age 90, or similar). Over 40 years, at 8% compounded, the $10,000 grows to $217,000.

But that same $10,000, invested at the same 8%, but being dragged down by 30% tax each year, grows to just $88,000!

That is not a mistake. Here are the calculations.

---

[6] https://www.morningstar.com/funds/when-bad-taxes-happen-good-funds

To calculate the future value, compounding once a year, we take the 8%, and add 1. That gives us 1.08. We then take that 1.08 and raise it to the 40th power. That's easy to do on a calculator or spreadsheet. We find that 1.08 to the 40th power is 21.724. Multiply the initial $10,000 by 21.724, and we get $217,240.

We do the same thing again to calculate the effect of taxes. A return of 8% before a 30% tax is the same as a return of 5.6% after tax. (Because 30% of 8% is 2.4%, and when we subtract the 2.4% from the 8%, because it's taxed away, that leaves 5.6%). We take 5.6% and add 1, which gives us 1.056, and raise that to the 40th power. A calculator or spreadsheet will show you that 1.056 to the 40th is 8.842. We multiply by $10,000 and get $88,420.

Sources of Tax Drag

Tax drag arises from several sources, each affecting portfolio returns differently.

The first major contributor is the taxation of dividends and interest income. Ordinary dividends, such as those from most mutual funds, are taxed at an investor's marginal income tax rate, which can be as high as 40.8% at the federal level. In addition, 43 states impose a state income tax, which can run as high as 13.3% in California, and to almost 15% for people living in New York City.

Interest income, for example from taxable bonds or bank deposits, faces the same tax treatment.

The second major source is capital gains taxes. Short term capital gains, that is gains on investments held for less than one year, are taxed at the ordinary income rate. Long-term capital gains are taxed at a lower rate. As of this writing, the Federal rate for long term capital gains goes up to 20%.

Trading within a portfolio can trigger short-term gains, resulting in an effective increase in the tax burden. For example, an investor realizing $50,000 in short-term gains at a 35% tax rate would owe $17,500 in taxes, whereas the same gain taxed as a long-term gain at 15% would result in a $7,500 tax bill—a savings of $10,000 by being taxed at long-term rates.

State and local taxes also amplify the effects of tax drag, particularly in high-tax jurisdictions. For instance, an investor in California could face taxes exceeding 50% on an account that earned mostly short-term gains.

Another significant but often overlooked source is mutual fund distributions. Even if an investor does not sell shares, mutual funds may distribute taxable capital gains to shareholders at year's end. These distributions can create unexpected tax liabilities, reducing the net return for investors holding these funds in taxable accounts.

Quantifying the Long-Term Impact of Tax Drag

Let's take a look at several reasonable scenarios, and quantify the potential tax drag for each of them.

First, consider an investor with $1,000,000 in a portfolio earning a 7.2% gross annual return. Without tax drag, the portfolio would grow to approximately $4 million over 20 years.

Assume, as is generally the best case, that all the returns earned are long term capital gains or qualified dividends. And let's also assume the investor is in an average state tax environment, so that the effective tax rate is 30%. If the tax is incurred every year as the returns are earned (not a bad assumption for many accounts), the tax drag wallops the ending value.

After taxes, instead of the $1 million quadrupling to $4 million in twenty years, in year twenty the investor will have only $2,670,000. That's a loss of over $1,300,000.

THE CATASTROPHIC CASE OF HIGH TURNOVER

When taxable accounts are invested in strategies that require high turnover, taxes devastate long term compounding. High turnover has the dual effects of causing all gains to be realized each year and therefore taxed, and also of causing the tax rate to be the short-term capital gain rate, which at the federal level tops out at 40.8%.[7]

Consider the results if, as above, the exact same pre-tax return of 7.2% were earned, but the turnover resulted in the gains being taxed at short term rates and state taxes of 6.2% (about the average) for a total tax rate of 47%, the tax drag would be even more destructive. Instead of having $4

---

[7] As of this writing, 37% federal plus 3.8% Obamacare or Net Investment Income ("NII") tax, summing to 40.8%.

million after twenty years, the investor would have only $2,110,000, for a loss of almost two thirds of the gain!

And for high performing, high turnover funds, such as some hedge funds, the tax drag can be even more devastating.

Consider a fund that earns an average of 10% for 20 years. That is excellent performance, but taxes can devastate it. Before taxes, $1 million would grow to $6.73 million. But if the fund is owned in a taxable account where the gains are taxed at 47% each year, the initial $1 million invested grows to only $2.81 million. Taxes reduced the gain by $3.92 million. Who are you investing for: yourself or the government?

FREQUENTLY SUGGESTED STRATEGIES FOR MINIMIZING TAX DRAG

There is a certain amount of conventional wisdom regarding the reduction of tax drag. Some of this wisdom makes sense, and some of it doesn't.

It is frequently suggested that an effective strategy is to concentrate high-drag-producing assets, such as taxable bonds, in tax-deferred accounts, especially retirement accounts like IRAs and 401ks.

Another strategy might be to weigh the portfolio in favor of investments that are expected to be more tax efficient, such as equities over bonds.

Tax-loss harvesting is another potentially useful tool. By selling losing investments to realize losses, it may be possible to offset taxable gains elsewhere in the portfolio. For example, realizing $10,000 in losses from one position to offset $10,000 in gains can save an investor in the 25% tax bracket $2,500 in taxes. Reinvesting the proceeds in a similar but not identical security ensures the portfolio remains aligned with its investment objectives while capturing the tax benefit.

Investment vehicle selection also plays a critical role in reducing tax drag. ETFs generally offer superior tax efficiency compared to mutual funds because of their unique in-kind redemption process, which minimizes taxable distributions. For investors who prefer mutual funds, tax-managed funds are designed to reduce turnover and avoid distributing gains unnecessarily.

DON'T LET THE TAIL WAG THE DOG – MUNI BONDS

Much of the conventional approach to minimizing tax drag incurs the risk of having the tax tail wag the investment dog. A particularly common example of this is the use of tax-exempt municipal bonds. In today's environment, investing in muni bonds for tax reasons may be a mistake.

As you probably know, interest from most municipal bonds is exempt from federal tax under IRC § 103(a), which excludes interest on municipal bonds from federal income tax.

Hidden Risk?

This is not a treatise on muni bonds. However, especially if you are considering owning long term muni bonds, you should be aware that the tax exemption for muni bonds (according to the IRS and most authorities) exists at the whim of Congress (and is not in the constitution). There is in principle no reason that the federal government could not seek to impose its will on states or localities by threatening to, or by actually removing, the tax-exempt status of muni bonds. The federal government routinely uses its spending power (e.g. see "§ 384.401 Withholding of funds based on noncompliance") to cudgel states into doing what the feds want. In government thinking, not-taxing something is the same as spending money (they call it a "tax expenditure") so the idea of taxing munis, or threatening to do so, is likely always lurking in the background.

The total value of muni bonds outstanding was, in 2024, about $4.1 trillion. As an extremely rough approximation, assume that all that debt, if taxable, would yield an average of 5%. That would equate to $200 billion of interest. If it were taxed at 32%, that would represent about $64 billion a year. That amount is comparable to many so-called "tax expenditures."

Beware of "Equivalent Taxable Yield"

Muni bonds are often marketed in terms of "equivalent taxable yield." But be very careful with such comparisons, because they can be misleading in at least two ways. First, the "equivalent taxable yield" is not an actual yield. You cannot earn it, and more importantly, you cannot compound it.

Second, muni bonds are often incorrectly compared to taxable bonds of higher credit quality.

Consider for example a generic investment grade 10 year muni bond. The yield is about 3%. Compare this to the 10-year US Treasury, with a yield of about 4.4%.

The implied breakeven tax rate between the two is about 32%. And that ignores the fact that the muni bond portfolio almost certainly carries a higher level of default risk than the treasury bond. (The fact is that municipal bond credit analysis is a complex field really understood by a small group. If you are going to invest in munis, it almost certainly makes sense to do so only via a very widely diversified portfolio.)

The comparison also ignores compounding. Effective long-term investment relies on compounding. In most cases, it is better to compound a higher number, and pay taxes later, than to pay taxes up front and compound a lower number. This is the basic idea behind IRAs. You invest pre-tax earnings (because you can deduct the amount going into the IRA) compound for years or decades, and pay tax when you withdraw.

In the case of muni bonds, earning a lower rate each year is like paying tax each year.

Here's an example. Suppose an investor has $1 million. Invested at 3%, tax free, and compounded for 30 years, at the end the investor will have $2,427,000.

Compare that to investing the same $1 million, tax deferred for 30 years, at 4.4% compounded each year. The $1 million will grow to $3,639,000. Of that, $2,639,000 is taxable. The tax on the gain, at 32%, would be $844,000. That would leave the investor with $2,795,000.

In this example, investing at the higher rate and deferring the tax adds over $300,000 to the ending value.

SOLUTIONS

In this section, we will look at four of the most commonly used solutions to the problem of tax drag. Each of these solutions has its place.

Qualified Retirement Accounts

The term qualified retirement plan is widely used to refer to plans such as IRAs, 401(k)s, 403(b)s, 457s, and similar.

As of 2024, there was approximately $15 trillion in IRA accounts, about $7 trillion in 401(k) accounts, about a trillion in 403(b) accounts, and smaller amounts in other specialized plans.

Interestingly, technically most IRAs are not actually "qualified accounts" in the sense that IRAs are not governed by ERISA. IRAs are covered in section 408.

Roth and Regular

As most readers will probably know, there are two types of IRAs and 401(k)s – regular and Roth. Regular plans are funded with pre-tax income, and when the income is paid out, the increase in plan value is taxable as ordinary income. Roth plans, in contrast, are funded with after-tax dollars, and when income is paid out there is no further income tax.

Both types of plans can be excellent tax planning vehicles, especially for investors who do not expect to be pushed into higher tax brackets in their later years. Deciding between the Roth and regular versions should be guided mainly by the expectation of whether your current tax rate is higher or lower than the tax rate you expect when you withdraw. Traditionally, the expectation has been that people are in higher brackets when they are working, and will be in lower brackets when they retire. That may not hold true for high-net-worth investors.

For high-net-worth investors, the decision is mostly moot, because for both types of plans the limits on contributions mean that there is no meaningful ability to put new money into either type of plan.

Life Insurance

Life insurance is a vast field, to which people can and do devote their lives to understanding. Here we can do no more than outline the potential uses of life insurance as a tax preferred investing vehicle.

Qualifying life insurance policies can build up policy value (which can be tied to investment returns, as in a variable life policy) tax free.

The cost associated with variable life insurance should be studied. Variable life insurance commonly has some or all of the following costs:

Cost of insurance
Administrative fees
Mortality and expense risk charges
Surrender charges
Investment management fees
Option feature fees
Transaction fees

When there are expected to be severe adverse financial consequences of premature death, life insurance can be a valuable and appropriate tool. However, because life insurance is a risk shifting transaction, and the life insurance company must be paid to assume the risk, when there is no significant financial risk to be insured against, life insurance is likely to be significantly less compelling as a financial proposition.

Annuities

Variable annuities offer another tax-deferred investing option. Qualifying variable annuities can allow the investor to defer taxes on the growth of the amount invested in the policy. The main limitations that apply to variable annuities are the fact that all the gains in a variable annuity, when paid out, are taxable as ordinary income.

Variable annuities also come with annual charges, which can be significant. Nationwide Life Insurance Company estimates the annual fees as 2% to 3%.[8] That can be a significant hurdle to overcome.

TAX-EXEMPT TRUSTS

The ideal way to avoid tax drag would be if there were no taxes. But there are taxes. So, the next best solution is to hold your investments in a vehicle which is itself tax exempt.

---

[8] https://www.nationwide.com/lc/resources/investing-and-retirement/articles/annuity-prices#:~:text=While%20variable%20annuities%20generally%20have,income%20through%20optional%20riders%20or

That's why IRAs and 401(k)s are so popular. But you're very limited on how much you can put in, and everything you take out is taxed at high, ordinary rates.

What is a Tax-Exempt Trust?

The IRS code provides for certain types of trusts to be exempt from tax on the income earned by the trusts. Trusts that qualify under the proper sections are therefore tax-exempt trusts. They can be very valuable planning solutions for people who know how to use them properly.

Tax-exempt trusts offer a solution that overcomes both the big limitations of retirement plans – the facts that retirement plans have low limits on the amount that can be contributed to the plan, and the fact that retirement plans convert all income to highly taxed ordinary income.

No Contribution Limits

With a tax-exempt trust, you can put in as much as you want. There are no contribution limits. You could put in a million, ten million, twenty million, there's no limit.

And, you are not forced to take taxable withdrawals at any specific time, like you are with IRAs and 401(k)s. You can let your assets compound, tax-deferred, indefinitely.

Income Taxed More Favorably

There's no tax until you take income out of the trust. And when you do take income, that income comes out to you as capital gain, if that's how the trust earned it. If an IRA earns capital gain, when it pays that gain out to you, it comes out as ordinary income. But with a tax-exempt trust, capital gains stay as capital gains. That can save you 17% on every dollar of gain.

Avoid Capital Gains

Tax exempt trusts can even be funded with appreciated property, without you having to sell and realize the gain. That can be a huge benefit.

For example, a couple owns Apple stock in which they have $3 million. In their state, the combined federal and state tax on the gain if they sold would be $1 million. However, if they first put the stock into a tax-exempt trust, the trust can sell and avoid the tax.

Instead of losing $1 million to tax, and having only $2 million working for them, with the trust, they can have the entire $3 million working for them.

More Income

Because the tax-exempt trust doesn't pay income tax, and the couple only pays income tax when they receive income from the trust, using the trust can allow them, and their family, to enjoy twice as much income over the life of the trust, as compared to keeping everything the same, except they paid the $1 million tax up front.

Much Better than an IRA

For example, suppose you had $1 million of capital gain in an IRA. When that gain is paid out, you'd be taxed on it at ordinary income rates. The top federal rate on ordinary income is 37%. That same gain, in a tax-exempt trust, would remain as capital gain. When it was paid out to you, it would be taxed as capital gain. The top rate on capital gains is 20%.

For the exact same gain, with an IRA you'd pay $370,000 of tax, while with a tax-exempt trust, you'd pay only $200,000. That's a savings for using a tax-exempt trust.

	Qualified Retirement Accounts	Life Insurance	Annuities	Tax-Exempt Trusts
Avoids Current Taxation	Yes	Yes	Yes	Yes
Income Tax Deduction?	Regular Only	No	No	Yes
Taxability of Payouts	Ordinary Income	None on Death Benefit	Ordinary	Same as income earned by Trust
Limits on Funding	Yes, quite low	No	No	No
Typical	Low	High	High[9]	Low

---

[9] Insurance firm Nationwide estimates that the average cost of a variable annuity is 2-3% per year.
https://www.nationwide.com/lc/resources/investing-and-retirement/articles/annuity-

Costs				

prices#:~:text=While%20variable%20annuities%20generally%20have,income
%20through%20optional%20riders%20or

6. Taxation of Complex Trusts

A *complex trust* is any trust that does not meet the conditions to be a simple trust.

Simple Trust

A simple trust is a trust that must distribute all its income in the same year it receives the income. A simple trust cannot accumulate income, cannot distribute out of corpus (also called principal), and it may not distribute funds for charitable purposes. If a trust distributes corpus during a year, as in the year it terminates, the trust becomes a complex trust for that year.[10]

For many people, perhaps the most salient "simplicity" of a simple trust is the fact that the simple trust distributes its income, and therefore, you would expect, the trust itself would have no income and no tax.

Until 2017 and the enactment of the TCJA[11] law, it was pretty much a certainty that a simple trust wouldn't have to pay tax. However, due to changes in the deductibility of miscellaneous items, it is possible that a simple trust's distributable net income (DNI) can differ from its trust accounting income (TAI). Without going into the gritty details, it is possible that both trust accounting income and actual distributions can be less than distributable net income. When this is the case, the trust itself may owe income tax on the amount of distributable net income not actually distributed.

So much for "simple."

COMPLEX TRUSTS

As the above discussion suggests, even a "simple" trust might not be simple in the ordinary meaning of the word.

Similarly, just because a trust is a "complex" trust, it is not necessarily complex in the ordinary meaning of that word.

A Complex trust, by definition, is any trust which is not a "simple" trust.

---

[10] IRS Regs. Sec. 1.651(a)-1
[11] "Tax Cuts and Jobs Act"

There are a variety of distinguishable types of complex trusts. They are typically used when a trust is desired and a simple trust will not suit the purpose. Complex trusts can accumulate income, distribute principal, and make charitable contributions, among other features.

Taxation of Complex Trusts

The major rule to keep in mind for a complex trust is that "income required to be distributed currently" is deductible from the trust's taxable income.

For example, suppose a trust is required to distribute all its income each year to beneficiaries.

That income, then, would be deductible by the trust. It would also be taxable income to the beneficiaries receiving it.

Even if the trustee has discretion to "sprinkle"[12] income among several beneficiaries, if the income must be distributed it is deductible from the trust's income.

In addition to deducting income that must be distributed, a complex trust may generally deduct trustee fees and administrative expenses actually paid. Depending on the specifics of the trust, charitable contributions made by the trust may be deductible from the trust's income.

A "personal exemption" of $100 is allowed under §642(b).

TAX RATES FOR COMPLEX TRUSTS

Complex trusts are subject to the same tax brackets as individuals, but the higher rates take effect at much lower income levels. For tax year 2024, the highest federal income tax rate of 37% applies to trust income over $14,450. Additionally, trusts may be subject to the Obamacare or Net Investment Income Tax (NIIT) of 3.8% on investment income, adding to the tax burden.

Because of the higher rates at lower levels of income, the effective tax on income taxed to a complex trust can be significantly higher than the tax on the same income if earned by a couple. In an example we reviewed, the same $500,000 of income incurred about $50,000 more income

---

[12] A trustee's power to "sprinkle" is the trustee's authority to decide how, when (and even "why" though a trustee is rarely required to explain why when the trustee is given sprinkle powers) to distribute trust income among trust's beneficiaries

taxes in a complex trust as compared to the tax that would have been incurred had the couple paid tax on it personally.

Form 1041

Most complex trusts must file IRS Form 1041, U.S. Income Tax Return for Estates and Trusts, annually. This form reports the trust's income, deductions, gains, and losses, as well as the distributions to beneficiaries. The trust must also provide each beneficiary with a copy of that beneficiary's form K-1. The K-1 provides details of the recipient's share of the trust's income, deductions, and credits, thus allowing the beneficiary to report his or her share of the trust's income items on that beneficiary's personal tax return (generally form 1040).

State Taxes

In addition to federal taxes, complex trusts may be subject to state income taxes. State tax rules vary significantly, with some states imposing taxes based on the trust's residence, the trustee's residence, or the beneficiaries' residence. This complexity requires careful consideration of state tax laws in the trust's overall tax planning.

SOME USES OF COMPLEX TRUSTS

We've seen that in many circumstances, the total federal income tax on a given amount of income will be higher at the complex trust level than if the same income were earned by individuals.

But there are also a number of situations where this is not the case. Many of these situations apply to high-net-worth investors.

Family is in the Top Tax Bracket

Many high-net-worth families are also high-income families and are in the top tax bracket. In these cases, there is no additional tax cost of using a complex trust, and conceivably there could even be a savings of a few dollars, though that saving is unlikely to be material.

State Income Taxes

Forty-three states (as of 2024) have an income tax. Complex trusts may be arranged so that there is no state income tax on the income. In these cases, the use of a complex trust, if it avoids state income tax on the income, can actually generate a large, significant overall tax saving.

Non-Tax Reasons

There are many non-tax reasons to prefer using a complex trust, including the desire to provide for charity, to provide discretionary distributions, to protect certain assets, and to take care of special needs.

7. Generation-Skipping Tax Trap

The generation-skipping tax is an estate tax on steroids.

It is essentially a double tax. Generation-skipping tax is imposed on gifts or other non-exempt transfers (the rules are complex, and we're just outlining them here) to someone other than a child who is more than 37.5 years younger than the giver.

The tax rate on Generation Skipping Tax is currently 40%. This tax is in addition to the estate tax.

The tax can be challenging to understand, and even more challenging when it cannot be avoided.

The effective tax rate on a taxable generation-skipping gift can be an astonishing 80%.

For example, suppose that a widow, Mrs. Generous, has no remaining estate or generation skipping exemption. She dies, leaving $1 million to her sole surviving heir, her granddaughter.

Her granddaughter is considered a "skip" person, and because Mrs. Generous has no remaining exemption, the entire $1 million is subject to both the estate tax, and the generation-skipping tax.

Each of those taxes is 40%, on the entire $1 million. The estate tax, therefore, will be $400,000. The generation-skipping tax is also $400,000. After paying those taxes, the estate retains only $200,000, which is what the granddaughter receives.

That's an effective tax rate of 80%!

EXEMPTIONS

Until the scheduled sunset of the 2017 tax law at the end of 2025, each US citizen currently has a lifetime estate and gift tax exemption of $13.6 million (which will be approximately $14 million in 2025).

The sunset, if it takes effect as scheduled on January 1, 2026, will reduce that exemption to about $7 million.

The same exemption amounts apply to the generation skipping tax.

SIMPLE EXAMPLE

The simplest way to apply an exemption is to make a gift to a person, and apply the appropriate exemption.

For example, suppose that Mrs. Jennifer Generous (known to her friends as Jen I) gives a gift worth $1 million dollars to her daughter, Jennifer, known as Jen II. It doesn't matter whether the gift is cash, or assets valued at $1 million. Jen I makes the gift, and when she files a gift tax return (form 709), she applies $1 million of estate/gift tax exemption.

The gift is tax free.[13] Jen I owes no tax on the gift. Jen II owes no tax on receiving the gift.

Now suppose that Jen II several years later gives $1 million to her own child, whom she has creatively named Jennifer. Everyone calls this person Jen III. That gift too, can be a tax-free gift, provided that Jen II has enough remaining lifetime exemption.

Jen II gives $1 million to Jen III. Jen II files a gift tax return, and uses $1 million of her lifetime exemption.

A BETTER WAY TO USE EXEMPTION

If the total value of the assets given from one generation to the next is significantly less than the lifetime exemption, the way that the Generous family did it in the above example will not create any tax, and there's probably no strong reason not to do it that way.

No one in the example has used a Generation Skipping Tax Exemption, but because there was no "skip" the set of transfers didn't result in generation-skipping tax.

However, there's probably a better way, and that becomes especially important as the value of the assets gets bigger.

---

[13] Tax-free with respect to the gift, estate, and generation-skipping taxes. Any income taxes that might be associated with the asset, such as capital gains, will not be eliminated. The general rule in a case like this is that the recipient of the gift inherits the giver's tax basis for purposes of capital gains taxes.

The Better Way

The better way is to apply both gift/estate tax exemption, and a corresponding amount of Generation Skipping Tax (GST) exemption.

To apply that GST exemption will, in general, involve a trust.

Trusts that are designed to have GST exemption applied to the assets given to the trust are usually referred to as Generation Skipping Trusts. You will sometimes hear the term "GST" applied to those trusts. It might be a bit confusing, because "GST" can refer to both the Generation Skipping Tax and the trusts designed to avoid that tax, called a Generation Skipping Trust. If someone uses the term "GST" and you're not sure what they mean, it's probably a good idea to ask.

Generation Skipping Trusts

A Generation-Skipping Trust allows assets to be transferred to descendants of the grantor, including those at least two generations below the grantor, such as grandchildren, and later descendants, while avoiding the estate tax and the generation-skipping tax.

The trust must be drafted correctly, and when the trust is funded, the appropriate amounts of the estate tax and GST exemptions must be applied.

When done correctly, the entire assets in the Generation-Skipping Trust are then exempt from estate or generation skipping tax for far into the future.

Avoiding a $143,000,000 Opportunity Loss

For the wealth creator who wishes to build long term wealth for his or her family, the proper use of a Generation Skipping Trust can make a giant difference in the long run.

Let's consider an example. Suppose that each generation has children 30 years apart. For simplicity, let's assume the following.
1. The lifetime exemption (for estate tax and GST) stays at today's $13.6 million.
2. Gen 1 passes $13.6 million to Gen 2 today. There's no tax.

3. Gen 2 invests the $13.6 million at an annual 5%, compounded, after income taxes.[14]
4. After 30 years, Gen 2 transfers the assets to Gen 3, and pays estate tax at 40% on the amount over the exempt amount.
5. Gen 3 grows the net after-tax amount it receives, and after 30 years passes that to Gen 4.

Given these assumptions, Gen 4 will receive $111 million in year 60. That's a lot of money, but it represents a compound, after-tax growth rate of only 3.5%. That 3.5% is actually slightly lower than the average inflation rate in the United States since 1933 when Franklin Roosevelt reneged on the government's pledge to exchange dollars for gold at a fixed rate. (For a detailed discussion of the history and causes of inflation, see *Politicians Spend, We Pay*, by Roger D. Silk, published by Sterling Lifetime Press, 2022.)

In contrast, if the two estate taxes -- one at year 30 and another at year 60 -- could be avoided, Gen 4 would receive not $111 million, but $254 million!

HOW TO SAVE $143 MILLION DOLLARS

Using the same facts as the above example, but avoiding the two incidences of the estate tax, Generation 4 would have an additional $143 million when it inherits.

And avoiding those estate taxes is exactly what a properly structured Generation Skipping Trust does.

In addition to avoiding confiscatory estate taxes, a properly structured Generation Skipping Trust can provide asset protection, provide for multiple generations, offer the family (or whoever the grantors determine are the right people) significant flexibility and control to adapt to situations as they develop in the future.

CUSTOMIZING THE SOLUTION

There are many potential customizations that investors, advisors, and attorneys may employ. We mention only four here.

---

[14] For thoughts on how to defer income taxes, please contact Sterling Foundation Management, LLC for a copy of a free Guide to tax-deferred compounding.

Distribution Trustee

All generation skipping trusts are irrevocable. A so-called spendthrift provision is common in irrevocable trusts.

A spendthrift provision protects the trust's assets from being seized by creditors of a beneficiary. But the spendthrift won't help if the beneficiary receives a payment from the trust. When the beneficiary receives a payment, a creditor of that beneficiary may be able to seize or lien the funds that have just come into the beneficiary's hands.

Suppose a beneficiary is his own trustee. While that might sound like a good thing, if the beneficiary has a creditor, it could turn out to be a bad thing. The creditor may be able to compel (through the courts) the beneficiary to distribute assets to himself, that the creditor would then legally take.

Investors, or their attorneys and advisors who are cognizant of this type of risk, might use a Distribution Trustee. A distribution trustee is a trustee whose only role is to decide, in that trustee's sole and absolute discretion, whether, when, and how much to distribute to a beneficiary. In the case of a beneficiary who has a creditor waiting to pounce on cash or assets distributed to the beneficiary, it may be much more difficult to compel a distribution trustee to distribute assets to the beneficiary.

Trust Protector

Some states allow a trust to have a role called trust protector. Depending on the law and how the trust is drafted, the trust protector can have the ability to hire and fire the trustee, without actually being the trustee.

Master LLC

A Master LLC is not part of a trust. Instead, it is an LLC that may own part of or all of the assets of the trust.

This can be useful for a variety of reasons. A Master LLC can have a single person, who is not a trustee, effectively manage the assets of the trust. It can be administratively easier to administer the assets of the trust via an LLC, as opposed to having the trust directly own assets. Even if a trust has multiple sub-trusts (e.g. a subtrust for each sibling or other family member), the assets held in a Master LLC can all be managed together.

Asset Diversification Trust

A generation skipping trust helps with estate, gift and GST tax avoidance, but on its own does little or nothing for income taxes. A tax-exempt asset diversification trust can hold part or all the assets of a generation skipping trust, and there is no income tax on those assets as long as the assets are owned in the asset diversification trust.

8. State Death Taxes: Trusts Can Help

Does your state impose a death tax, separate from the Federal estate tax? If you're not sure, you can find out below.

Most people are aware that the US federal government imposes an estate tax on large estates. As of 2025, there is a lifetime exemption per person of just under $14 million.

But not everyone is aware that 17 states (and the District of Columbia) also impose some sort of death tax.

This post provides an overview of the state death tax rules, and gives a shorthand estimate of the rates, exemption amounts, and expected changes.

Death Taxes: "Estate" Tax and "Inheritance" Tax

Technically, an estate tax is a tax levied on the estate itself, while an inheritance tax is levied on the heirs who inherit from the estate.

An inheritance tax tends to be more complicated to explain and analyze (as compared to the estate tax), because it falls on the inheritor. So, for example if a person has 10 heirs, the inheritance tax might affect each one differently.

The review follows.

STATES WITH ESTATE TAXES

Connecticut
 Exemption Amount: $13.61 million (2024), indexed for inflation.
 Tax Rates: Flat 12%.
 Expected Changes: None known.
District of Columbia
 Exemption Amount: $4.71 million (2024).
 Tax Rates: 11.2% to 16%.
 Expected Changes: None announced.
Hawaii
 Exemption Amount: $5.49 million (2024).
 Tax Rates: 10% to 20%.
Expected Changes: None announced.
Illinois
 Exemption Amount: $4 million.
 Tax Rates: 0.8% to 16%.
 Expected Changes: None announced.
Maine
 Exemption Amount: $6.8 million (2024).
 Tax Rates: 8% to 12%.

Expected Changes: None announced.
Maryland
    Exemption Amount: $5 million.
    Tax Rates: 0.8% to 16%.
    Expected Changes: None announced.
Massachusetts
    Exemption Amount: $2 million.
    Tax Rates: 7.2% to 16%.
    Expected Changes: None announced.
Minnesota
    Exemption Amount: $3 million (2024).
    Tax Rates: 13% to 16%.
    Expected Changes: None announced.
New York
    Exemption Amount: $6.94 million (2024).
    Tax Rates: 3.06% to 16%.
    Expected Changes: None announced. ("Cliff" system)
Oregon
    Exemption Amount: $1 million.
    Tax Rates: 10% to 16%.
    Expected Changes: None announced.
Rhode Island
    Exemption Amount: $40,000
    Tax Rates: 0.8% to 16%. Top rate effective over 1.774 million (2024)
    Expected Changes: None announced.
Vermont
    Exemption Amount: $5 million (2024).
    Tax Rates: 16%.
    Expected Changes: None announced.
    Washington
        Exemption Amount: $2.193 million (2024).
        Tax Rates: 10% to 20%.
        Expected Changes: None announced.

STATES WITH INHERITANCE TAXES

Iowa
    Exemption Amount: Varies based on the beneficiary's relationship to
    the decedent.
    Tax Rates: 5% to 15%.
    Expected Changes: The tax is being phased out and will be fully
    repealed by 2025.

Kentucky
>Exemption Amount: Varies based on the beneficiary's relationship to the decedent.
>Tax Rates: 4% to 16%.
>Expected Changes: None announced.

Maryland
>Exemption Amount: Varies based on the beneficiary's relationship to the decedent.
>Tax Rates: 10%.
>Expected Changes: None announced.

Nebraska
>Exemption Amount: Varies based on the beneficiary's relationship to the decedent.
>Tax Rates: 1% to 18%.
>Expected Changes: None announced.

New Jersey
>Exemption Amount: Varies based on the beneficiary's relationship to the decedent.
>Tax Rates: 11% to 16%.
>Expected Changes: None announced.

Pennsylvania
>Exemption Amount: Varies based on the beneficiary's relationship to the decedent.
>Tax Rates: 0% to 15%.

Expected Changes: None announced.

STATES WITH BOTH ESTATE AND INHERITANCE TAXES

Maryland
>Exemption Amount (Estate Tax): $5 million.
>Tax Rates (Estate Tax): 0.8% to 16%.
>Exemption Amount (Inheritance Tax): Varies based on the beneficiary's relationship to the decedent.
>Tax Rates (Inheritance Tax): 10%.
>Expected Changes: None announced.

EASY WAY TO AVOID ESTATE AND INHERITANCE TAX IN ALL BUT CONNECTICUT

Only Connecticut has a gift tax. So, in each of the other states, you can avoid the death tax by making gifts during life.

Easy Way to Make a Gift

Gifts to avoid state estate taxes do not necessarily have to be made directly to an heir. The gifts can be to a trust. Note that in general gifts must be made before death, and in some cases, there is a "clawback" period for gifts made within a certain amount of time, such as three years, of death.

Some of these trusts can be mainly for the goal of avoiding state death taxes. Others may avoid both state death taxes and home state income taxes. And yet others may allow the grantor to avoid state death taxes and income taxes, and also federal income taxes.

And in some cases, the gifts can be made in such a way that the giver can retain access and/or control over the assets gifted.

9. Incomplete Gift Non-Grantor Trusts ("ING")

Owners of small and medium size businesses in many high tax states may be able to sharply cut their state income taxes using a technique known as an incomplete gift non-grantor trust.

Incomplete gift non-grantor trusts (sometimes referred to as "INGs", or "NINGs" or "DINGs" or "WINGs" – we'll explain these odd terms below) are designed to help owners of high-income producing businesses and assets reduce state income tax liability, while protecting their wealth, and providing for their future and their heirs. Unlike most non-grantor trusts, incomplete gift non-grantor trusts are intentionally structured to ensure that the gift to the trust is considered incomplete for federal gift tax purposes, while the trust itself is treated as a non-grantor entity for income tax purposes.

An incomplete gift is not taxable for gift and estate tax purposes, so an incomplete gift will not trigger such taxes. However, as the trust is a non-grantor trust for income tax purposes, income earned by the trust will not flow to the grantor.

This structure, if it is permitted by state law, allows a grantor to shift income from a high-tax state to a low-tax or no-tax state, thereby reducing or eliminating state-level income tax on trust income.

No State Income Tax

Incomplete gift non-grantor trusts are typically established in jurisdictions with favorable trust laws, such as Delaware, Nevada, or Wyoming, which do not impose income tax on trust assets and offer flexible, robust trust administration frameworks. As with all tax and estate planning, incomplete gift non-grantor trusts should be carefully structured and administered to ensure that they comply with the Internal Revenue Code, and applicable state tax laws.

Non-Grantor

An incomplete gift non-grantor trust is an irrevocable trust that is intentionally designed to qualify as a non-grantor trust under the federal tax rules. The fact that the trust is a non-grantor trust means that the trust itself, rather than the grantor, is the taxpayer for income tax purposes.

Thus, the trust's income will be subject to taxation at the federal lever, at trust tax rates.

In addition, the trust income will, in general, be subject to state income tax in the state where the trust is, and not (in general) in the grantor's state of residence. If, as is usual, the trust is established and maintained in a state that does not tax trust income (such as Nevada, Delaware and Wyoming), there will be no state income tax on the trust's income.

As you may have guessed, a "NING" is a Nevada incomplete gift non-grantor trust, while a "DING" is one domiciled in Delaware, and a "WING" is one in Wyoming.

Grantor Can Be Beneficiary

The grantor can be a beneficiary of the incomplete gift non-grantor trust. This allows the grantor to access trust funds if needed, while allowing the funds to remain outside the grantor's home state for tax purposes if not needed. Note, however, that if the grantor does access the income, that income is likely going to be included in the grantor's state income, and therefore subject to state income tax.

Incomplete Gift

As the term incomplete gift non-grantor implies, the gift to the trust is considered incomplete for federal gift tax purposes. This is accomplished by the grantor retaining certain powers or interests in the trust that prevent the transfer of assets to the trust from being treated as a completed gift under gift tax rules. These retained powers typically include the right to veto distributions from the trust or the right to direct the trust's investments. By structuring the transfer as an incomplete gift, the grantor avoids triggering gift tax liability at the time the assets are transferred to the trust.

Example

Incomplete gift non-grantor trusts don't work in all circumstances. But to see how it can work, let's consider a simplified example.

Suppose Smith owns $20 million of assets that produce $1,000,000 a year of taxable income. Smith lives in a state that has a 10% state income tax rate.

Smith, in addition to owing federal income tax on the $1,000,000, will also owe $100,000 additional in state income taxes.

If Smith doesn't want to give the asset away (e.g. to children, or a trust for the benefit of children), an incomplete gift non-grantor trust might be a solution.

For example, if Smith sets up a Nevada incomplete gift non-grantor trust, and transfers the assets to the trust, Smith will no longer owe tax on the $1,000,000 of income. Instead, Smith's incomplete gift non-grantor trust will owe tax on the income.

Because Nevada does not have a state income tax, and does not tax trusts, Smith's trust owes only the Federal tax. No state income tax is due. Smith, or Smith's trust, saves the $100,000 of state tax.

Limitations

The approach is not without limitations or complexity. For example, not all states recognize the validity of the incomplete gift non-grantor trust. California and New York are two high tax states that have passed laws to tax the grantor on the income earned by such trusts.

The federal tax rates on trusts reach their highest rates at relatively low levels of income. For most high-income people, this is more of an annoyance than a decision changer.

Until 2020, it was possible to get the IRS to issue a private letter ruling on whether a particular trust design would satisfy the IRS's requirements for an incomplete gift non-grantor trust. But the IRS has stopped issuing such rulings.

Giving Up Control is Required to Make a Trust a Non-Grantor Trust

The rules for determining whether a trust is or is not a grantor trust are complex, and this is just an outline of some of the highlights. The main source of the rules is IRS code sections 671-679, and corresponding regulations. Important provisions include the following. A trust may be a grantor trust (and hence the trust's income will flow through to the grantor for tax purposes) if any of the following is the case.

(1) The grantor retains a reversionary interest. Section 673 of the code says, "The grantor shall be treated as the owner of any portion of a trust in which he has a reversionary interest in either the corpus or the income therefrom, if, as of the inception of that portion of the trust, the value of such interest exceeds 5 percent of the value of such portion." A reversionary interest means that the grantor will eventually get the property back.

(2) The grantor or non-adverse party has certain powers. The code says in part, that the grantor should not retain "power of disposition, exercisable by the grantor or a nonadverse party, or both, without the approval or consent of any adverse party." The IRS regulations define an adverse party at length, in 1.672(a)-1.

(3) The grantor has certain administrative powers, exercisable without the approval of an adverse party, such as the power to dispose of trust assets for less than fair market value, or borrow from the trust without adequate security, or certain "powers of administration" over the trust exist under which the grantor can or does benefit under Section 675.

(4) The grantor retains the power to revoke the trust.

(5) The grantor or a nonadverse party retains the power to distribute income to the grantor or the grantor's spouse.

Retaining Control is Required to Make a Trust an Incomplete Gift

The grantor must retain some powers, or the assets contributed to the trust will be considered a complete gift, and a gift tax return (and potentially gift taxes) will be required.

The basic idea seems to be that if the grantor retains the power to redirect who gets what, the gift will be incomplete. To give you a flavor of the clarity (or lack thereof) of the regulations, consider the following excerpt from regulation 25-2511-2:

As to any property, or part thereof or interest therein, of which the donor has so parted with dominion and control as to leave in him no power to change its disposition, whether for his own benefit or for the benefit of another, the gift is complete. But if upon a transfer of property (whether in trust or otherwise) the donor reserves any power over its disposition, the gift may be wholly incomplete, or may be partially complete and partially incomplete, depending upon all the facts in the particular case. Accordingly, in every case of a transfer of property subject to a reserved power, the terms of the power must be examined and its scope determined. For example, if a donor transfers property to another in trust to pay the income to the donor or accumulate it in the discretion of the trustee, and the donor retains a testamentary power to appoint the remainder among his descendants, no portion of the transfer is a completed gift. On the other hand, if the donor had not retained the testamentary power of appointment, but instead provided that the remainder should go to X or his heirs, the entire transfer would be a completed gift. However, if the exercise of the trustee's power in favor of the grantor is limited by a fixed or ascertainable standard (see paragraph (g)(2) of § 25.2511-1), enforceable by or on behalf of the grantor, then the gift is incomplete to the extent of the ascertainable value of any rights thus retained by the grantor.

As complicated as the law is, these laws are actually quite clearly understood by those who deal with them regularly. Good legal counsel can provide good guidance.

DISTRIBUTION POWER

For an incomplete gift non-grantor trust to qualify as such, the grantor cannot control distributions. Distributions must be consented to by an adverse party. To satisfy this requirement, often a distribution committee is vested with the power of determining distributions. The committee may include the grantor, but the committee must act with a majority of adverse parties.

The code, Sec 672, defines an adverse party. An excerpt: "the term "adverse party" means any person having a substantial beneficial interest in the trust which would be adversely affected by the exercise or nonexercise of the power which he possesses respecting the trust."

WHEN TO USE AN ING

An ING can allow a grantor to avoid state income taxes on income generated outside the grantor's home state. The most common sources of such income are investment income, such as that generated by a portfolio of securities. Another common source is the sale of a business.

To avoid home state taxes, the assets producing the income must be transferred to the ING trust before the income is generated.

Example – Sale of a Business

Suppose Jones owns a business that is expected to sell for $25 million. Jones' basis is zero, and he lives in a state with a 10% income tax rate. Upon sale, everything else equal, Jones would owe $2,500,000 in state income taxes, in addition to federal capital gains tax.

To avoid state tax by use of an ING, Jones would have to create the ING, and transfer ownership of the business to the ING, well in advance of a transaction. There are various reasons for this in-advance requirement, including making sure the transfer to trust is not disregarded, is not considered to be an assignment of income, is not treated as a sham, and similar considerations.

10. Stock Diversification Trusts

A stock diversification trust is a tax-exempt, irrevocable, non-grantor trust that meets certain qualifying tests. Appreciated stock can be contributed to a stock diversification trust tax-free, and the trust can then sell the stock, immediately, with no tax due. The trust then can reinvest the entire proceeds into a diversified portfolio. Furthermore, as long as the assets remain in the trust, there is no tax on income or capital gains realized by the trust. In addition, the contributor of stock to a stock diversification trust may receive a tax deduction for at least ten percent of the value of the assets contributed.

WHEN AND WHY TO USE

A stock diversification trust is typically used to diversify a concentrated stock holding. While there's no universally accepted quantitative definition of a concentrated, many financial experts consider a position concentrated when it represents 5% or more of an investor's total portfolio value.

The concept of diversification has ancient roots, with even biblical texts advising spreading investments across multiple ventures. In today's complex financial landscape, holding a concentrated position can expose investors to substantial risks.

The primary danger of a concentrated position is the potential for significant loss if the concentrated holding experiences a loss. Individual stocks almost always exhibit higher volatility compared to diversified portfolios.

Historical examples of risky stocks demonstrate that even well-established companies can experience severe losses. General Motors faced multiple 50% drops before its eventual bankruptcy. Netflix lost nearly 80% of its value in less than a year in 2022. General Electric, once considered a safe investment, has seen a 70-80% decline since 2000.

Modern finance theory focuses on portfolio-level risk rather than individual stock risk. It suggests that while it's challenging to consistently earn "excess" returns above market averages, investors should aim to avoid "excess" risk – risk beyond what's necessary to achieve expected returns.

Concentrated positions typically introduce excess risk without a corresponding increase in expected returns. Author James Grant, in a slightly different context, referred to this, tongue-in-cheek, as a case of "return-free risk." That is, by holding concentrated positions, investors are taking additional risk for which, according to finance theory, they cannot reasonably expect to get paid. By diversifying, investors can potentially reduce portfolio volatility without sacrificing long-term performance.

EXAMPLE

Consider a situation in which a 70-year-old owns $5 million of Microsoft stock with essentially zero basis. His unrealized gain is $5 million. He lives in Washington state, which has a 7% state income tax on capital gains. In addition, he is in the top federal bracket. Overall, if he sells, he will owe taxes equal to 30% of the gain. That is, selling stock will cost him $1.5 million in tax, leaving him with only $3.5 million. It's taken him the better part of forty years to amass the $5 million, but the government will claim $1.5 million the day he sells. Doesn't seem fair.

To make it fairer, he can contribute the $5 million of Microsoft stock to a properly structured stock diversification trust. The contribution is not taxable, and the trust could immediately sell the stock, recognizing the entire $5 million. The trust would owe no tax, and so it would have $5 million to invest in a diversified portfolio of assets. Now, the entire $5 million can be invested. The grantor and his wife can receive 5% of the trust value as income each year, for as long as they live. After the second of them dies, their two children will share the income for as long as they live.

In addition, the contributor would receive an income tax deduction of at least $500,000 in the year the stock was put into trust.

QUALIFYING THE TRUST

To qualify as a tax-exempt trust, stock diversification trust must meet certain rules.[15] Key among these rules is that the contributor retains the right to an income stream, not less than 5% per year, from the trust for a period that can last a very long time. The exact length of the income period depends upon a number of factors, but generally is not more than about sixty years.

The trust is irrevocable, and the grantor gives up the right to the trust principal, and keeps the right to the income stream. At the end of the trust term, which will usually be well after the end of the contributor's life, the balance remaining in the trust can be used to establish a charitable legacy for the contributor.

---

[15] The full rules are in §664 of the Internal Revenue Code. These rules have been present since 1969.

ASSET PROTECTION

In addition to the tax benefits of a stock diversification trust, because it is an irrevocable trust, a stock diversification trust can include asset protection language which under certain circumstances will protect the trust assets from any claims that might be brought against the trust income beneficiaries. This extra benefit comes for free if the trust is properly drafted.

ABILITY TO PROVIDE FOR CHILDREN, GRANDCHILDREN

A stock diversification trust can be structured so that after the original grantor (and spouse) dies, the grantor's children can receive the income. In some cases, even the grantor's grandchildren can be in line to receive income. There is no stated maximum possible term for a trust, but the expected life of most stock diversification trusts would be in the range of fifty to sixty years.

PAYOUTS AND TRUST TERM

The stock owner who contributes stock to a stock diversification trust can decide who is eligible to receive payouts from the trust. Typically, the owner will retain the right to receive payouts, usually 5% of the trust value each year, for life. The owner's spouse can also be a beneficiary, and in the vast majority of cases the trust can last for at least the longer of the spouses' lives.

In addition, in most cases, the owner and/or spouse can also name one or more children, or nieces or nephews (or anyone, really) to be a successor income beneficiary. In some cases, depending on the ages involved, grandchildren can also become beneficiaries after their parents and grandparents are no longer living.

The expected term of most stock diversification trusts is determined by the length of the lives of the beneficiaries, and by reference to actuarial tables. In the typical case, the expected life of the trust will be 50 to 60 years. At the conclusion of the trust term, the trust assets can be used to fund a legacy charitable endowment, which can be administered by the owner's grandchildren and subsequently by great grandchildren, ad infinitum.

DEFERRAL POTENTIAL

A properly constructed and properly managed stock diversification trust can provide a period of tax-free deferral during which no payments are made to the beneficiaries, and instead the assets grow, inside the trust, tax-free.

When this deferral is in place, the trustee maintains a bookkeeping account called an accumulation account. Each year while deferral is occurring, the amount that would have been eligible to be paid, but wasn't, is added to the accumulation account.

For example, if a trust could have paid out $50,000 a year, but is in deferral mode for five years, after five years there would be $250,000 in the accumulation account. If after five years deferral was no longer desired, this accumulated amount could then be paid, in whole, or in part, in one year or over multiple years. In addition, the annual payment from the trust could be paid on top of the accumulated amount.

DEFERRAL IS A POWERFUL COMPOUNDING TOOL

Almost everyone is familiar with the wealth-building value of tax deferral. The entire $20 trillion plus retirement investment industry is built on the foundation of tax deferral. A simple example illustrates the power of deferral.

Assume an investor has $1 million growing at an annual rate of 5% over 40 years. We'll compare two scenarios: one with tax-deferred growth and one where gains are taxed annually at 30%. If taxes are paid each year, (as, for example, if the income were paid out of the trust each year), this cuts the effective annual growth rate to 3.5% per year,[16] and the value at the end would be $3,959,360.[17]

However, if everything is the same, except the income is not paid out each year, the original $1 million would grow to $7,039,989, almost double! Just from tax deferral.

At higher rates of return, the effect is even more pronounced. For example, at 8%, taxed each year at 30%, $1 million would grow to about $10,285,000. But deferring the tax would allow the account to reach $21,724,000 at the end of forty years. If the 30% tax were then paid on the gain of $20,724,000, the after-tax amount would still be over $15,500,000!

---

[16] Effective Growth Rate = 5% $\times$ (1 - 0.30) = 3.5%

[17] Future Value = $1,000,000 $\times$ $(1 + 0.035)^{40}$

54

Merely by deferring tax, the after-tax amount is about $5 million greater than it would be if tax were paid each year.

WEALTH BUILDING POWER OF TAX DEFERRAL

In the last example above, the tax-deferred account grows to approximately $15.5 million after taxes, while the taxable account grows to about $10.3 million. The difference of roughly $5 million illustrates the compounding advantage of tax deferral, allowing more capital to remain invested over time. This significant gap underscores the long-term benefit of deferring taxes, especially in high-return environments over extended periods.

PROFESSIONAL MANAGEMENT

Stock diversification trusts should be managed by professionals. The management is frequently split between a trustee who attends to all the trust-specific compliance, accounting, reporting, and tax returns, and an investment manager who handles the investments.

TAX REPORTING

A stock diversification trust is a separate tax-reporting entity. Even though the trust itself is tax exempt, it must file tax returns. These returns might be quite complex, but such complexity does not affect the income beneficiary.

Each income beneficiary will receive a tax form k-1 from the trust. These forms are typically one page of information.

TAX TREATMENT OF PAYMENTS

Section 664 provides that a stock diversification trust keep track of four "buckets" of income. These buckets, roughly speaking, are 1) ordinary income 2) long-term capital gains 3) tax-exempt income and 4) trust capital.

When a trust earns income, that income goes (in an accounting sense) into the appropriate bucket. When the trust makes a payment to an income beneficiary, the tax law says that those payments are deemed to come first from ordinary income, until that bucket is empty, then from long-term capital gain until that bucket is empty, and so on.

LIMITATIONS

The income beneficiaries of a stock diversification trust do not have access to trust principal. For example, if an owner contributes $1 million to a trust, that owner will have the right to the income payout, usually 5%, for life, and the life of a spouse, and then potentially the lives of one or more children, and even grandchildren. But the trust principal itself no longer belongs to the owner.

LIQUIDITY

The stock diversification trust itself must be irrevocable. That means that after the grantor contributes stock to the stock diversification trust, the grantor goes from owning the stock outright to owning the right to a stream of payments from the trust.

This stream of payments is a capital asset. One characteristic of capital assets is that they can generally be sold, and gains from sale are treated as capital gains.

In the case of stock diversification trusts, a properly drafted trust can allow the grantor (or subsequent income beneficiary) to sell an income interest, thereby generating liquidity in excess of the annual income stream, if necessary. There is a secondary market for streams of trust income, and under some circumstances it is possible to sell this right.

KEY DECISIONS

Once you've decided to use a stock diversification trust, there are four main, easy, decisions to make:
1. Do you want to be an income beneficiary?
2. Do you have a spouse who you want to be a successor income beneficiary?
3. Who do you want to be income beneficiaries after you and/or your spouse?
4. What property (e.g. shares of stock) do you want to contribute to the trust for the trust to sell, without tax, and reinvest?

11. Crypto Diversification Trusts

Cryptocurrency has created unparalleled opportunities for wealth generation, transforming early adopters into multimillionaires seemingly overnight. The meteoric rise of Bitcoin, Ethereum, and other digital assets has rewarded bold investors who recognized the potential of blockchain technology. However, this newfound success comes with significant challenges, especially for those looking to capitalize on their gains without eroding their wealth.

"Tokens" Not "Currency"

While it is common to use the phrase "cryptocurrency" we prefer the terms "crypto" or "crypto token" because so far to date, few if any cryptos actually function as currencies.

In the view of economists, cryptos lack key characteristics of traditional currencies. Most crucially, to be money, by definition, an asset must be the most liquid and widely accepted commodity in exchange in an economy. While there might exist some very small, specialized communities in which a particular crypto is the de-facto currency, because it is the most accepted asset in exchange, in the observable economy, no crypto functions that way.

To economists, regulators, and taxing authorities, cryptos are property. The majority view is that cryptos are speculative assets rather than functioning currencies.

Some crypto advocates believe that crypto, or at least Bitcoin, will become a currency, it is not in economic terms a currency now. And, for US people, perhaps the more relevant fact is that the IRS treats crypto tokens as capital assets.[18] That is important, because it means that gains on crypto are capital gains. For most people in most circumstances, gains on currency are taxed as ordinary income under section 988.

MARKET CAPITALIZATION

At the end of 2024, the total market capitalization of all crypto tokens exceeded $3 trillion. While small compared to the market cap of global real estate, estimated to exceed $300 trillion, or the global bond market cap which exceeds $100 trillion, crypto is now about 1/3rd the size of the total gold market cap, and exceeds the estimated market value (about $1.4 trillion at $25 per ounce) of all the world's silver

---

[18] IRS Notice 2014-21

Volatility

Cryptocurrencies are renowned for their significant price volatility, often surpassing that of traditional financial assets. This volatility is typically measured using metrics such as the 30-day annualized volatility, which reflects the degree of price fluctuation over a 30-day period, annualized for comparison purposes.[19]

High But Declining

Bitcoin's historical volatility shows extreme fluctuations, particularly in its early years. Between 2010 and 2013, Bitcoin's 30-day annualized volatility frequently exceeded 100%, with peaks reaching as high as 150%, driven by the speculative nature of the nascent market.

From 2014 to 2017, as the market began maturing, volatility started to decrease but remained elevated, ranging between 50% and 100%.

The period between 2018 and 2021 saw further gradual decline, with the 30-day annualized volatility typically staying below 80%, though it could still spike sharply due to significant market events or regulatory announcements.

More recently, from 2022 to 2024, Bitcoin's volatility further diminished, generally remaining below 60%, attributed to increased institutional adoption, market maturation, and the introduction of financial instruments like exchange-traded funds (ETFs) that stabilize investment flows.

Despite these reductions, Bitcoin's volatility remains higher compared to traditional assets like equities or fiat currencies. For example, major stock indices such as the S&P 500 typically exhibit annualized volatility between 15% and 20%, which is considerably lower than Bitcoin's.

Volatility in Practice

Despite the general downward trend in Bitcoin volatility, volatility remains a real challenge for investors. For example, in 2021, Bitcoin surged to an all-time high of $69,000 in November, only to plummet by over 70% to below $20,000 within a year. Ethereum experienced a similar rollercoaster ride, peaking at over $4,800 before dropping below $1,000 in the same timeframe. Such swings can wipe out millions of dollars in

---

[19] In most cases, the reported number is the daily standard deviation of return, annualized. If you really want to dig into this, be aware that while the standard practice in financial markets is to annualize daily volatility by multiplying by the square root of 252 (because there are typically 252 trading days in the financial markets), the crypto markets trade every day of the year, and therefore daily volatility of crypto is often annualized by using the square root of 365. For comparison, the square root of 252 is about 15.9 and the square root of 365 is about 19.

portfolio value in mere weeks, leaving even seasoned investors grappling with anxiety and uncertainty.

TAXES

For those who decide to sell to lock in gains, a different kind of problem arises: taxes. In the United States, the federal capital gains tax on long-term investments is up to 20%, with an additional 3.8% net investment income tax for high earners. State taxes can push the total rate above 30% in some jurisdictions, and up to 37.1% in California, and even higher for some residents of New York.

For short-term holdings, the tax burden is even greater, aligning with ordinary income tax rates that can reach 37% plus 3.8%, and again, state income taxes are on top of these already very high rates. For short term gains in high tax states, it can mean that selling $5 million worth of appreciated cryptocurrency could result in more than $2.5 million, over half the gain, lost to taxes.

A TIGER BY THE TAIL

These twin dilemmas—crypto's extreme volatility and the painful bite of taxes—leave many investors feeling trapped. Holding onto assets in a volatile market could lead to massive losses, but selling them could mean surrendering a significant portion of hard-earned gains to the taxman.

This is the reality that many successful crypto investors face: a feeling of a no-win scenario where wealth preservation feels almost impossible.

THE COMPLEXITY OF SELLING APPRECIATED CRYPTO

Consider Sarah Thompson, a fictional yet representative investor who purchased $100,000 worth of Ethereum (ETH) in 2018. By 2024, her portfolio had grown to an astonishing $3 million. While this incredible growth positioned her for financial freedom, it also presented Sarah with difficult decisions. She wanted to sell her Ethereum to diversify into safer, income-generating assets, but the thought of losing over $1 million in taxes was unbearable. Sarah also felt in her bones that holding onto her ETH indefinitely carried immense risk. After all, she had already experienced the value of her ETH drop by over 75%.

Sarah's situation is not unique. Thousands of crypto investors find themselves in similar situations, struggling to balance risk management with tax efficiency. Traditional alternatives, like selling and paying taxes, or borrowing against assets, each have significant drawbacks. For Sarah, the stakes were high, and she needed a solution that would allow her to sell without sacrificing her financial future.

BORROWING

While it may be technically feasible to borrow against certain crypto tokens, the volatility of crypto rules out borrowing as a long-term solution for most holders in most situations. The reason is that because volatility is so high, a very high ratio of collateral is likely to be required for each dollar lent.

For example, using recently available data from the "Decentralized Finance" or "DeFi" markets, it would be possible to borrow 50% of the value of your ETH holdings. A typical lender might set a collateral threshold of 82.5% of the initial collateral.

The $3 million of ETH would allow you to borrow $1.5 million by posting the entire $3 million of collateral. The lender would then set a "threshold" value of $2,475,000 on the ETH posted. So, if the value of your ETH dropped below $2,475,000, the lender would have the right to sell it. Selling it would pay off your loan, but it would also lock in your loss, and cause you to realize the gain and owe taxes.

Probability of Loan Dropping Below Threshold

It turns out that we can use the historical data on volatility to estimate the probability of the loan dropping below the thresholds, and therefore the probability that you could be forced out of your loan and forced to recognize the gain. Assuming that historical annualized standard deviation of return on ETH is about 92%, and that continues to be the volatility going forward, there is about a 30% risk that the collateral will drop below the threshold in one year. The longer the loan is outstanding, the greater the risk.

INTRODUCING THE CRYPTO DIVERSIFICATION TRUST

For most people, there is a much better alternative. For investors like Sarah, a Crypto Diversification Trust[20] offers a compelling

---

[20] The Crypto Diversification Trust was developed and perfected by Sterling Foundation Management, LLC, based in Reston, Virginia.

alternative. This tax-exempt trust allows individuals to sell appreciated cryptocurrency, without incurring immediate capital gains taxes. By transferring assets into a Crypto Diversification Trust, investors can unlock the value of their crypto holdings without paying tax, secure a steady income stream, and provide for a long-term legacy —all while preserving more of their wealth.

In Sarah's case, establishing a Crypto Diversification Trust transformed her financial outlook. She transferred her $3 million in Ethereum into the trust, avoiding the $1.05 million in capital gains taxes she would have owed. The trust then sold the Ethereum tax-free, allowing Sarah to reinvest the full proceeds into a diversified portfolio of income-generating assets.

From the Crypto Diversification Trust, Sarah received an annual income that started at $150,000, giving her the financial security she needed to transition out of the volatile crypto market. That income is expected to grow as the trust assets, invested wisely, also grow over time. Sarah's asset in trust is also protected from potential creditors, should any arise.

WHY THE CRYPTO DIVERSIFICATION TRUST WORKS FOR CRYPTO INVESTORS

The Crypto Diversification Trust's appeal lies in its ability to address the core challenges faced by crypto investors. First, it eliminates the immediate tax liability associated with selling appreciated assets. By leveraging the tax-exempt status of the trust, investors can sell without losing a significant portion of their wealth to capital gains taxes.

Second, the Crypto Diversification Trust provides an extremely valuable ability to reduce market risk by diversifying out of crypto without having to pay tax to do so. Once the crypto is sold within the trust, the proceeds can be reinvested into a diversified portfolio, reducing exposure to the dramatic swings of the crypto market. This approach allows investors to lock in their gains, and move their wealth into a far less volatile form.

In addition, once the assets are in the trust, the investment manager can readjust the portfolio as needed, without needing to pay much attention to the tax consequences. This is because the trust is tax-exempt, and when the trust realizes gains or income, the trust does not pay tax on those gains or income.

The Crypto Diversification Trust provides a flexible, tax-deferred investment vehicle that can provide income for decades, for up to three generations, and finally will create a legacy for the grantor that can last forever.

THE LONG-TERM BENEFITS OF A CRYPTO DIVERSIFICATION TRUST

For Sarah, the Crypto Diversification Trust was a game-changer. For the rest of her life, she'll be entitled to 5% income from the trust, which started at $150,000. Her trust is invested mostly in the markets, with an expected long run rate of return of 8%. At that rate, her income will grow at 3% a year.

Sarah continues to work, and doesn't need the entire $150,000 each year. Her advisor works with her, and in most years little of the $150,000 is actually distributed. Instead, it remains in the trust, pre-tax, and compounds, meaning that Sarah's future annual income from the trust is growing much more rapidly.

Beyond Sarah's personal story, the Crypto Diversification Trust model has helped and continues countless crypto investors navigate the complex interplay of taxation, volatility, and wealth preservation. For those who have reaped significant rewards from the crypto market, the Crypto Diversification Trust offers a way to protect and grow wealth, ensuring that success in the digital asset space translates into long-term financial security.

12.   Special Needs Trusts

For families with loved ones who have disabilities, financial planning is more than just managing money—it's about ensuring lifelong care, dignity, and security. The challenge is often daunting: How do you provide for a loved one without jeopardizing essential government benefits? How do you make sure that care continues even after you're gone? These are the questions that keep parents, siblings, and caregivers awake at night. The solution, for many, is a Special Needs Trust.

A Special Needs Trust isn't just a financial tool; it's peace of mind in legal form. It allows families to set aside money and assets to care for someone with special needs without disqualifying that person from government benefits like Medicaid or Supplemental Security Income (SSI). These benefits can be a lifeline, covering crucial services that private funds alone may never fully provide. But the eligibility rules are strict. A single financial misstep—like an inheritance paid directly to the beneficiary—can lead to the loss of those benefits, leaving vulnerable individuals without critical care.

The fundamental issue is that government programs have strict asset limits. For example, as of this writing a person receiving SSI must have less than $2,000 in countable assets to remain eligible. Anything above that amount could disqualify them. It's a heartbreaking reality: Families who want to leave money to ensure their loved one's future can inadvertently do more harm than good by giving them direct access to funds. This is where the Special Needs Trust comes in.

Example

Take the case of David and Susan, parents of a son named Ethan who has autism. Ethan requires ongoing support, including specialized therapy, housing assistance, and help with daily living activities. His parents have always worried about his future, particularly what will happen when they are no longer around to care for him. They've saved diligently, hoping to leave enough money to cover his needs. But when they spoke with their financial advisor, they discovered a problem: Leaving a traditional inheritance to Ethan would put his government benefits at risk.

SPECIAL NEEDS TRUST

A special needs trust is a legal arrangement designed to provide financial support for individuals with disabilities or chronic illnesses while preserving their eligibility for essential government benefits. This type of trust allows a physically or mentally disabled person to receive income and maintain assets while still qualifying for public assistance programs such as Medicaid, Supplemental Security Income (SSI), and Social Security. If the individual received the assets directly, the income might disqualify the person for the taxpayer provided aid.

The primary purpose of a special needs trust is to enhance the quality of life for the beneficiary by supplementing, rather than replacing, the basic support provided by government programs. These trusts are typically used to cover expenses that are not covered by public assistance payments, such as medical expenses, caretaker payments, and transportation costs.

TWO TYPES

There are two main types of special needs trusts: third-party trusts and first-party trusts. A third-party special needs trust, also known as a supplemental needs trust, is funded with assets belonging to someone other than the beneficiary. This could include gifts, inheritances, or life insurance proceeds. On the other hand, a first-party trust is funded with the beneficiary's own assets, often from personal injury settlements or inheritances received directly by the beneficiary.

As with most trusts, a special needs trust involves three key roles: the grantor, the trustee, and the beneficiary. The grantor is the person who creates the trust and provides the initial funding. The trustee is responsible for managing the trust assets and making disbursements according to the trust's terms. The beneficiary is the person with special needs for whom the trust is established.

PURPOSE

The primary reason for most special needs trusts is that such a trust allows the beneficiary to maintain eligibility for needs-based government programs. These programs often have strict income and asset limits, and without a special needs trust, direct financial support could disqualify an individual from receiving crucial benefits. By placing assets in a properly structured trust, the beneficiary can enjoy additional financial support without exceeding these limits.

TRUST TERMS

Special needs trusts are typically irrevocable, meaning that once established, they cannot be easily changed or revoked. This irrevocable nature provides an additional layer of protection for the beneficiary, as the assets held in the trust cannot be seized by creditors or by the winner of a lawsuit.

When establishing a special needs trust, it is advisable to carefully define the terms of the trust document. The language used must be precise and technical to ensure that the trust funds are not considered the beneficiary's own property. This precision is necessary to maintain the beneficiary's eligibility for government benefits. Each state may also have its own laws, so advice from competent counsel is highly advised.

The trust document should also include specific instructions about the individual's needs and how the trust funds can be used. This level of detail allows for a highly personalized approach to meeting the beneficiary's unique requirements while ensuring that the trust remains compliant with federal and state regulations.

FUNDING

Special needs trusts can be funded in various ways. Common funding sources include gifts from family members, inheritances, proceeds from life insurance policies, and settlements from personal injury lawsuits. It is important to note that for third-party trusts, funds belonging to the beneficiary should not be used to fund the trust, as this could potentially compromise the trust's effectiveness in preserving benefit eligibility.

MANAGEMENT

While it is common for the trustee of a special needs trust to manage the trust assets, make investment decisions, and distribute funds in accordance with the trust's terms, it is not required that all these functions be performed by a single role. It is possible (and may be desirable in some situations) to have the administrative responsibilities of the trustee separate from the investment management.

The distribution role typically involves understanding of the beneficiary's needs, as well as knowledge of the rules governing public assistance programs. The trustee must exercise discretion in making distributions to ensure that the beneficiary's eligibility for government benefits is not compromised. The administrative functions require knowledge of the relevant tax, accounting and compliance rules. These are conceptually separate from the investment role.

PAYMENTS TO MEDICAID

First party special needs trusts require that the funds eventually be used to repay Medicaid. One of the key advantages of a third-party special needs trust is that there is no payback requirement to Medicaid upon the beneficiary's death. This means that any remaining funds in the trust can be distributed to other beneficiaries as specified in the trust document. This feature makes third-party trusts an attractive option for parents or other family members who wish to provide for a loved one with special needs while also preserving assets for other heirs.

When considering the establishment of a special needs trust, it is important to evaluate the likelihood that the beneficiary will need means-tested benefits either now or in the future. If there is a possibility that the individual may require Medicaid or other similar programs, a special needs trust can be a valuable tool in preserving eligibility while providing additional support.

USES OF FUNDS

The funds in a special needs trust can be used for a wide variety of purposes to improve the beneficiary's quality of life. Common expenses covered by these trusts include educational costs, recreational activities, counseling services, and medical attention beyond the basic necessities provided by government programs. The trust can also pay for items such as electronic equipment, furniture, vacations, and other comforts that public assistance does not typically cover.

TRUSTEE SELECTION

It is important to note that special needs trusts are subject to specific rules and regulations. For example, the trust must be established before the beneficiary turns 65 years old. Additionally, the beneficiary cannot serve as the trustee of their own special needs trust, as this would be considered to give them control over the assets, potentially jeopardizing their eligibility for government benefits.

When creating a special needs trust, careful consideration should be given to the selection of trustees and the balance of power within the trust structure. Given that these trusts often remain in effect for many years, sometimes spanning generations, it is crucial to think about who will serve as trustee and what powers they will have. Some families choose to appoint family members as trustees, while others opt for corporate trustees or a combination of both.

PROTECTOR

To provide additional oversight and protection for the beneficiary, some trusts include provisions for a trust protector or trust advisor. A trust protector is typically an independent third party who has the power to make certain changes to the trust or remove and replace trustees if necessary. A trust advisor, on the other hand, may provide guidance to the trustee on matters relating to the beneficiary's care and needs [8].

Special needs trusts can also offer protection against financial abuse. Individuals with certain disabilities may be at higher risk of exploitation, and by placing assets in a trust with a responsible trustee overseeing disbursements, the beneficiary's financial resources are better safeguarded.

GOVERNING LAW

It is important to understand that special needs trusts are governed by both federal and state laws. In the United States, the primary federal statute governing special needs trusts is found in Title 42 United States Code Section 1396p(d)(4)(A). Many states have also established their own statutes regarding the creation and use of special needs trusts. To be valid, a special needs trust must comply with both federal and applicable state requirements.

The use of special needs trusts extends beyond the United States. Several common law nations have established specific statutes related to the creation and use of these trusts. This international recognition underscores the importance of special needs trusts as a tool for providing financial support to individuals with disabilities while preserving their access to essential government benefits.

One of the challenges in managing a special needs trust is ensuring that distributions from the trust do not inadvertently disqualify the beneficiary from receiving government benefits. Certain types of distributions, particularly those that could be construed as providing for food or shelter, may be counted as income by government agencies and could potentially reduce or eliminate the beneficiary's eligibility for programs like SSI. Trustees must be well-versed in these rules and exercise caution when making distributions [1][8].

TAX AND ESTATE IMPLICATIONS

Another important consideration in the administration of a special needs trust is tax planning. The tax implications of a special needs trust can be complex and depend on various factors, including the type of trust (first-party or third-party), the nature of the distributions, and the overall financial situation of the beneficiary. It is often advisable to work with a tax professional who has experience with special needs trusts to ensure compliance with tax laws and to optimize the trust's tax efficiency.

When establishing a special needs trust, it is crucial to coordinate the trust with other estate planning documents and beneficiary designations. For example, if parents create a special needs trust for their child but fail to update their wills or the beneficiary designations on their life insurance policies and retirement accounts, the intended protection of the trust may be compromised. It is important to review and update all relevant financial and legal documents to ensure that assets flow into the special needs trust as intended.

Special needs trusts can also play a role in long-term care planning. As individuals with disabilities age, their care needs may change, and the costs of care may increase. A well-structured special needs trust can provide a flexible source of funds to meet these evolving needs while preserving eligibility for government programs that may cover basic care costs.

POOLED TRUSTS

In some cases, families may consider using a pooled trust as an alternative to an individual special needs trust. Pooled trusts are managed by nonprofit organizations and combine the resources of many beneficiaries for investment purposes while maintaining separate accounts for each beneficiary. These trusts can be a good option for smaller estates or situations where finding an appropriate individual trustee is challenging.

It is worth noting that while special needs trusts offer many benefits, they are not the only option for providing financial support to individuals with disabilities. Other strategies, such as ABLE accounts (Achieving a Better Life Experience), can complement or, in some cases, serve as an alternative to special needs trusts. ABLE accounts offer tax-advantaged savings opportunities for individuals with disabilities, with some similarities to 529 college savings plans.

The field of special needs planning is continually evolving, with changes in laws, regulations, and best practices occurring regularly. Families and trustees involved with special needs trusts should stay informed about these developments and be prepared to adapt their strategies as needed. This may involve periodic reviews of the trust document and distribution practices to ensure ongoing compliance and effectiveness.

13.   Real Estate Shelter Trusts

A Real Estate Shelter Trust is an irrevocable, tax-exempt trust. Contributions of appreciated real estate to such a trust are tax-free, and the trust can then immediately sell the real estate with no tax due. The trust then can reinvest the entire proceeds into a diversified portfolio. Furthermore, as long as the assets remain in the trust, there is no tax on income or capital gains realized by the trust. The grantor, and up to three generations of the grantor's family, may receive income from the trust. In addition, the contributor of real estate to a Real Estate Shelter Trust may receive a tax deduction for a portion of the value of the assets contributed.

CASE STUDY: HARRY LYONS

Harry Lyons, a 71-year-old apartment investor, had long enjoyed success in real estate. However, with the arrival of his grandchild, he began considering slowing down to spend more time with family. Managing his properties became more burdensome than rewarding. Initially, Harry contemplated a tax-free exchange into lower-maintenance triple-net leases, but the government's COVID-related eviction moratorium accelerated his decision to act.

Frustrated by the CDC's intervention in landlord-tenant agreements, Harry sought alternatives to reduce his real estate exposure. Harry contacted Sterling Foundation Management, the creator of the Real Estate Shelter Trust, to explore options that would align with Harry's goals of reducing risk, diversifying investments, and simplifying his life.

After discussions, Harry emphasized his frustration with tenant nonpayment during the moratorium. He saw concentrated real estate holdings as an "excess risk" that left him exposed. Tax implications also loomed large. His properties, acquired in the early 1990s in Phoenix with a cap rate of about 7%, had appreciated significantly, now valued at around $15 million. However, his adjusted tax basis was nearly zero, and depreciation recapture, combined with capital gains taxes, would trigger a $4.5 million tax bill upon sale. "I'd rather die!" Harry exclaimed at the thought of such a liability.

Holding the properties until death for a stepped-up basis wasn't a viable solution given Harry's desire to enjoy life now. Harry, being a seasoned real estate investor, knew all about 1031 exchanges. He rejected a 1031 exchange because he wanted to diversify out of real estate, and 1031 requires that you keep all your capital in real estate.

Harry chose to create and fund a Real Estate Shelter Trust with Sterling. This approach allowed him to create two tax-exempt trusts, providing income for him and his wife, then continuing for his children.

Lyons Roar LLC was formed to hold Harry's properties. Upon sale, it realized over $15.1 million, now invested in a diversified portfolio. Harry can draw up to $756,000 annually, with payments deferred to reduce immediate tax liability. The trust ensures growth, benefiting his family for generations.

WHY DIVERSIFY BEYOND REAL ESTATE

Excess Risk in Concentrated Real Estate Holdings

Since ancient times, investors have understood that diversification helps reduce risk. Modern Portfolio Theory (MPT), pioneered by Harry Markowitz, mathematically demonstrates that a well-diversified portfolio can lower risk without compromising expected returns. While MPT has primarily focused on stocks and bonds due to their frequent trading and available data, the theory applies to real estate as well. However, analyzing real estate risks presents unique challenges due to limited transaction data, especially for privately held properties.

From MPT's perspective, real estate is like any other asset class, and its risk can be assessed similarly. The critical difference between publicly traded real estate, such as Real Estate Investment Trusts (REITs), and privately owned properties is liquidity. Publicly traded assets can be sold quickly with minimal transaction costs. In contrast, private real estate, including apartment buildings, takes weeks or months to sell and incurs higher costs.

Some investors perceive privately owned real estate as safer than publicly traded REITs, but this assumption is flawed. Consider two identical apartment complexes—one owned by a publicly traded REIT and the other privately held. Both properties face the same economic risks. Yet, reports from promoters of private real estate frequently claim private real estate has significantly lower risk, a notion stemming from data provided by the National Council of Real Estate Investment Fiduciaries (NCREIF).

NCREIF data shows smoother, less volatile returns for private real estate compared to publicly traded REITs. However, experts like Peter Linneman[21] argue that this perceived stability is misleading, resulting from data inaccuracies rather than actual lower risk. Linneman contends that

---

[21] Peter Linneman, *The Return Volatility of Publicly and Privately Owned Real Estate*, Wharton Working Paper #493, Review.

the methodology used to analyze private real estate data understates its volatility.

Ultimately, owning concentrated real estate holdings carries risks akin to concentrated stock positions. Individual properties, like individual stocks, are inherently risky due to their lack of diversification. Despite this, real estate owners often hesitate to sell due to significant tax liabilities, creating a barrier to diversification.

Concentrated real estate holdings expose investors to excess risk, emphasizing the importance of diversification to manage those risks effectively. As with stocks, reducing concentration in real estate can help mitigate risk, even though tax considerations often complicate the decision to sell and diversify.

THE TWO SOURCES OF TAXABLE GAINS ON REAL ESTATE

In the U.S., at the federal level, real estate sales are subject to taxes on two types of gains: appreciation in the property's market value and gains from depreciation recapture. Many states also impose taxes.

The first source of taxable gain is the increase in a property's market value between purchase and sale. For instance, a property bought for $1 million and sold for $2.2 million results in a $1.2 million gain, which is taxed at capital gains rates. As of this writing, the top federal capital gains rate is 23.8%, with an average state tax rate of 6.2%, making the combined top rate around 30%. However, inflation impacts the real gain, as a property must appreciate just to keep pace with rising prices. For example, over a decade ending in 2022, inflation eroded the dollar's value by 22%, meaning a $1 million property in 2012 would need to be worth $1.275 million in 2022 just to break even. Despite this, the government taxes the inflationary gain, effectively imposing a hidden tax.

The second source of taxable gain arises from depreciation recapture. Depreciation reflects the economic decline in an asset's value due to wear, usage, and obsolescence. For tax purposes, businesses can deduct depreciation from their income, reducing taxable income. In real estate, depreciation applies to buildings, not land, with residential buildings depreciated over 27.5 years and commercial buildings over 39 years.

When a property is sold, previously deducted depreciation must be "recaptured" and taxed. Depreciation recapture on real property is taxed at 25%, plus a 3.8% surtax for high-income earners, totaling 28.8%. Depreciation on certain components, such as HVAC systems, may be taxed at ordinary income rates if a cost segregation method was used.

For example, a $3 million apartment building with $2.75 million in depreciable property would generate about $100,000 in annual depreciation. After ten years, the owner's basis would be $2 million. If the property were then sold for $3 million, the owner has no real gain but must pay depreciation recapture taxes on the $1 million depreciation taken. At 28.8%, this results in a $288,000 tax bill. If faster depreciation methods like cost segregation were used, parts of the depreciation could be taxed at ordinary income rates, further increasing the tax liability.

Depreciation recapture creates a significant tax burden for real estate investors, even in cases where there is no real gain on the sale, making it a crucial consideration in tax planning for the sale of real estate.

Real Estate Shelter Trust

A Real Estate Shelter Trust is often the best solution for an investor selling real estate, because the trust can allow the seller to avoid gain on the sale.

To qualify as a tax-exempt trust, the trust must meet certain rules.[22] Key among these rules is the rule that the contributor retains the right to an income stream, not less than 5% per year, from the trust for a period that can last a very long time, but generally not more than about sixty years. The contributor gives up the right to the trust principal, and keeps the right to the income stream. At the end of the trust term, which will usually be well after the end of the contributor's life, the balance remaining in the trust can be used to establish a charitable legacy for the contributor.

Asset Protection

In addition to the tax benefits of a Real Estate Shelter Trust, because it is a trust, a Real Estate Shelter Trust can include language designed to protect the trust assets from any claims that might be brought against the trust income beneficiaries. This asset protection benefit can be combined with the tax benefits of the Real Estate Shelter Trust.

Ability to Provide for Children, Grandchildren

A Real Estate Shelter Trust can be structured so that after the grantor and spouse (if there was one) die, the contributor's children can receive the income. In some cases, even the contributor's grandchildren can be in line to receive income. There is no stated maximum possible term for a trust, but the expected life of most Real Estate Shelter Trusts is in the range of fifty to sixty years.

---

[22] The rules are in section 664 of the Internal Revenue Code.

Payouts and Trust Term

The property owner who contributes stock to a Real Estate Shelter Trust can decide who is eligible to receive payouts from the trust. Typically, the owner will retain the right to receive payouts, usually 5% of the trust value each year, for life. The owner's spouse can also be a beneficiary, and in the vast majority of cases the trust can last for at least the longer of the spouses' lives.

In addition, in most cases, the owner and/or spouse can also name one or more children, or nieces or nephews (or anyone, really) to be a successor income beneficiary. In some cases, depending on the ages involved, grandchildren can also become beneficiaries after their parents and grandparents are no longer living.

The expected term of most Real Estate Shelter Trusts is determined by the length of the lives of the beneficiaries, and by reference to actuarial tables. In the typical case, the expected life of the trust will be 50 to 60 years. At the conclusion of the trust term, the trust assets can be used to fund a legacy charitable endowment, which can be administered by the owner's grandchildren.

Deferral Option

A properly constructed and properly managed Real Estate Shelter Trust can provide a period of tax-free deferral during which no payments are made to the beneficiaries, and instead the assets grow, inside the trust, tax-free.

When this deferral is in place, the trustee maintains a bookkeeping account called an accumulation account. Each year while deferral is occurring, the amount that would have been eligible to be paid, but wasn't, is added to the accumulation account. For example, if a trust could have paid out $50,000 a year but is in deferral mode for five years, after five years there would be $250,000 in the accumulation account. If after five years deferral was no longer desired, this accumulated amount could then be paid, in whole, or in part, in one year or over multiple years. In addition, the annual payment from the trust could be paid on top of the accumulated amount.

Professional Management

Real estate shelter trusts should be managed by professionals. The management is frequently split between a trustee who attends to all the trust-specific compliance, accounting, reporting, and tax returns, and an investment manager who handles the investments.

Tax Reporting

A Real Estate Shelter Trust is a separate tax-reporting entity. Even though the trust itself is tax exempt, it must file tax returns. These returns might be quite complex, but such complexity does not affect the income beneficiary.

Each income beneficiary will receive a tax form K-1 from the trust. These forms are typically one page of information.

Tax Treatment of Payments

Section 664 provides that a Real Estate Shelter Trust keep track of four tiers or categories of income. These tiers, roughly speaking, are 1) ordinary income 2) long-term capital gains 3) tax-exempt income and 4) trust capital.

When a trust earns income, that income goes (in an accounting sense) into the appropriate bucket. When the trust makes a payment to an income beneficiary, the tax law says that those payments are deemed to come first from ordinary income, until that bucket is empty, then from long-term capital gain until that bucket is empty, and so on.

Limitations

The income beneficiaries of a Real Estate Shelter Trust do not have access to trust principal. For example, if an owner contributes $1 million to a trust, that owner will have the right to the income payout, usually 5%, for life, and the life of a spouse, and then potentially the lives of one or more children, and even grandchildren. But the trust principal itself no longer belongs to the owner.

In other words, after the owner contributes real estate to the Real Estate Shelter Trust, the owner goes from owning the real estate outright to owning the right to a stream of payments from the trust. This stream of payments is a capital asset. There is a secondary market for streams of trust income, and under some circumstances it is possible to sell this right.

Note: A significantly expanded version of this chapter is available free from Sterling Foundation Management to readers of this book. Email REST@SterlingFoundations, and mention this book and ask for the Real Estate Shelter Trust guide offer. This offer may be withdrawn at any time.

14. StretchIRA Trusts

A StretchIRA Trust is a carefully designed hybrid trust designed to protect most retirement plans from the ravages of the SECURE Act "death tax."

The SECURE Act (which like so many government laws has been given an Orwellian name" stands for "Setting Every Community Up for Retirement Enhancement." It introduced significant changes to how inherited retirement accounts are taxed, leading some to refer to it as a "death tax" on retirement savings.

One of the most significant changes brought by the SECURE Act is the elimination of the right of most non-spouse beneficiaries to elect to withdraw the retirement plan over their own remaining life expectancy. Before the SECURE Act, such beneficiaries could elect to "stretch" the payments, that is, to distribute inherited retirement account balances over their lifetimes, allowing for extended tax-deferred growth and potentially lower tax burdens. However, under the new rules, most beneficiaries are required to withdraw the entire balance of an inherited retirement account within 10 years of the original owner's death.

This 10-year rule has significant tax implications for beneficiaries. For example, if a beneficiary inherits a $1,500,000 IRA and is in the top federal tax bracket, it can cost an estimated $600,000 of income taxes because the entire plan must be withdrawn and taxes paid.

The accelerated distribution requirement can push beneficiaries into higher tax brackets during the 10-year period. As most people with large plans die in their seventies or eighties, their adult heirs are also likely to be in the prime earning years of their lives.

For example, an 82-year-old with a $1 million IRA dies, and his son and heir is 52. The son is already in a high tax bracket, and the IRA distributions are likely to be taxed at the highest rates, and even push the son into a higher bracket if there are any higher brackets.

This compression of distributions into a shorter timeframe often results in a larger overall tax burden for beneficiaries, hence the "death tax" moniker.[23]

To deal with this emergent problem of the Secure Act death tax, Sterling Foundation Management created the StretchIRA Trust.

---

[23] There are exceptions to the 10-year rule, including surviving spouses, disabled or chronically ill individuals, individuals not more than 10 years younger than the deceased, and minor children of the account owner (until they reach the age of majority).

TAX BENEFIT TO TAX TRAP

The successful investor who uses a regular retirement account, such as an IRA, 401(k), or 403(b), often ends up having created a large tax liability. For example, an investor who contributed the maximum amount to a personal IRA each year since 1980, and invested it in the S&P 500 would face a very steep tax upon withdrawal. That investor never contributed more than $6000 in any year, yet by the end of 2024 had over $2.5 million in his IRA account.

There are hundreds of thousands of IRAs and 401(k) accounts in this size range. According to IRS data, there are perhaps two million retirement accounts worth at least $1 million dollars.

These large retirement accounts represent, to the IRS, huge future tax revenues. The reason is that the entire balances of the accounts are subject to income tax at ordinary income tax rates, and in all but a few situations, the owners must begin withdrawals, and payment of tax, when they reach age 73.

Required Minimum Distributions

Required Minimum Distributions (RMDs) are the government's way of taking a large bite out of the hard-earned retirement savings of successful investors. For most IRA, 401(k), and 403(b) account owners, their required minimum distribution is calculated using Table III from Appendix B of IRS publication 590b. If you're not sure, check with your advisor, or refer to publication 590b, section titled "Which Table Do You Use to Determine Your Required Minimum Distribution."

Required Minimum Distributions are based on age, and work out to be a certain specified percentage (specified implicitly in the table) of the remaining asset value in the account at the beginning of the year. The table provides a number (roughly, the life expectancy at that age), and the RMD is calculated by multiplying the reciprocal of the table number by the year's beginning account balance.

For example, if the table number were 20, and the beginning of the year account balance were $1 million, the RMD would be
$$\$1,000,000/20 = \$50,000.$$

THE "STILL WORKING" EXCEPTION

Most people who reach the age at which RMDs begin (currently 73 as of this writing), must begin taking RMDs the year in which they reach that age.

However, a small group of people may not be required to take RMDs, even when they reach the age. People who are actively employed and have money in their current employer-sponsored retirement plan, like a 401(k), are generally allowed to delay taking Required Minimum Distributions (RMDs) from that employer plan while they are still working, until they retire, regardless of their age, as long as the employer plan doesn't mandate otherwise.

The still working exception is otherwise beyond the scope of this book.

Contact RMD@SterlingFoundations.com to learn more about RMDs and the still working exception.

Death and Taxes

Benjamin Franklin, commenting upon the new US Constitution, said "In this world, nothing is certain but death and taxes."

The Constitution Franklin was commenting on did not allow for an income tax. And in fact, for the first 140 years of the existence of this country, we got on fine without an income tax. But now we have one, and it hits retirement plans with a vengeance.

We saw above that if the investor survives to his expected life, with reasonable growth, he will withdraw and pay income taxes on the entire amount, and then some, with which he has in the plan at age 73.

But if he dies, the situation is no better. Unless the investor (or plan owner – different names for the same person) rolls the retirement plan to a spouse, the entire plan must be withdrawn and income taxes paid within ten years. And if the investor is married and dies, and the plan is rolled to the spouse, the outcome is often not much better, because the spouse must also take required minimum distributions, generally based on the same schedule.

IRA Spousal Rollovers

In the United States, the average married couple differs in age by about 2 years, with the man on average being older. We use that fact to examine the effect of a spousal rollover of an Individual Retirement Account, almost universally called an IRA.12 A surviving spouse can set up a "spousal rollover IRA" not only for IRA accounts, but also for 401(k)s and other plans, if the plan documents permit it. We will use the term IRA for simplicity.

Suppose for sake of discussion that the above man reaches 72 with $2.1 million in his retirement plan, and the plan account earns an average of 7%. Suppose he dies at age 75, when his wife is age 73. After taking his RMD, he dies and the plan has assets of $2,350,000.

His wife, age 73, must begin taking RMDs according to her schedule. Her Pub 590b Table I life expectancy is 15 years. We assume that she lives to her life expectancy, and the account earns an average of 7% per year.

Over the 15 years of her life expectancy, she will be required to take distributions totaling $2,516,000. She'll pay tax on all of that.

So even dying doesn't get the original plan owner out of a huge amount of income tax.

They got you coming and going, or so it seems. But there may be a few ways to have a better outcome.

SOLUTIONS, POTENTIAL SOLUTIONS AND NON-SOLUTIONS

Potential Solution: Still Working Exception

As noted above, for individuals who qualify, there is one solution to the problem of unwanted required minimum distributions. This solution is called the "still working exception."

The exception can apply to employees who are still working at the employer who holds their 401(k). The still working exception does not apply to IRAs, and does not apply to 401(k) accounts or 403(b) accounts that might be held at a former employer.

A further limitation on the still working exception is that it does not apply to employees who own, or used to own, 5% or more of the company.

Potential Solution: Qualified Charitable Distribution

For individuals who have an IRA and are required to take a minimum distribution, one potential solution is to have the IRA distribute an amount, up to $100,000 per year, directly to charity. A qualified charitable distribution (QCD) will not show up as income, nor will there be an income tax deduction. The downside, of course, is that the money is gone. So, a qualified charitable distribution only makes sense if the individual was going to give that amount of money to charity anyway.

In general, a qualified charitable distribution must go directly to an operating public charity. It cannot go to a private foundation or a donor advised fund account.

Potential Solution: Roth Conversion

A "Roth conversion" is a taxable withdrawal from an IRA that is rolled over into a Roth IRA. Some commentators seem to see a Roth conversion as a panacea, or a "must have" conversation. But while Roth conversions can make sense in some circumstances, those circumstances might not be very widely applicable.

In addition, the thorough investor (or the investor's advisor) might well find better solutions in many cases in which a Roth conversion is considered.

We're skipping the math here, but the math shows that if we take an "everything else equal" analysis, we find that a Roth conversion generally can be expected to make sense only if the plan owner's current income tax rate is lower than the future expected tax rate.

Even when that is the case, many people will defer the conversion because once a tax is paid, it can never be recovered. Many people just don't want to pay a tax now that they don't have to pay, even if it might, in the long run, end up saving them money.

And if an investor lives in one of the 41 states with an income tax, and may later move to one of the 9 states (Alaska, Florida, Nevada, New Hampshire, South Dakota, Tennessee, Texas, Washington and Wyoming) that do not tax retirement withdrawals, a Roth conversion could backfire.

Roth Conversions in the Real World

Do Roth conversions really work? James S. Welch found that, if done optimally, which involved a sophisticated technique from the field of operations research called linear programming, found that "partial conversions early in the optimal plan increase disposable income by around 1 percent."[24]

On an investor board[25] online, we found a discussion by a poster with screen name Indywho who had run a mixed integer program[26] to determine the optimal conditions for Roth conversion. Among other things, Indywho noted that his model had 2022 variables and 2580 constraints. Such a model, he said, had too many variables for excel to run, and he had to use a program called opensolver.

When all was said and done, he reported, the conversion still would take an estimated 20 years to breakeven, and the ultimate gain was relatively small.

Few investors, and few advisors, are in a position to confidently run a linear programming analysis, or a mixed integer analysis, even if they want to.

---

[24] *Measuring the Financial Consequences of IRA to Roth IRA Conversion*, Journal of Personal Finance, Vol. 5, Issue 1, 2016

[25] https://www.bogleheads.org/forum/viewtopic.php?t=286154

[26] Mixed Integer Programming is a class of optimization problems in which some variables are constrained to be integers, while others are allowed to take continuous (real-number) values. The objective is to maximize or minimize a linear function, subject to a system of linear equality and/or inequality constraints. If you don't understand this, don't worry. It's not likely to make a material difference in your life.

Life Insurance

We include life insurance in this discussion of RMD strategies because it is frequently mentioned (often by people who sell life insurance) as a recommended strategy.

One specific strategy mentioned is to take RMDs, pay the tax, and use the remaining amount to purchase life insurance. This strategy could take advantage of the special tax treatment of afforded life insurance, but there is nothing that we see that makes it unique or especially suited to RMD situations.

OUR PREFERRED SOLUTION: STRETCHIRA TRUST

A StretchIRA trust is a trust specially designed and developed by Sterling Foundation Management specifically for the situation in which owners of large retirement plans – IRAs, 401(k)s, 403(b)s, and similar, find themselves.

A StretchIRA trust is implemented during a plan owner's life, and named as the beneficiary of the plan, or plans. An owner can use a single StretchIRA Trust to be the beneficiary of multiple retirement plans, even of different types of retirement plans. For example, a person might have two IRAs and two 401(k)s, and name a single StretchIRA Trust as the beneficiary of all of the plans.

When a StretchIRA trust is named as the beneficiary of a retirement plan, upon the plan owner's death, the entire assets of the retirement account are paid, tax-free, to the StretchIRA trust. If the trust receives stocks or mutual funds, the trust can keep them, or sell and reinvest, immediately, with no tax due. Furthermore, as long as the assets remain in the trust, there is no tax on income or capital gains realized by the trust.

While the assets were in the retirement plan, not only were the assets subject to required minimum distributions, but all gains, regardless of source, were converted to ordinary income. Many large retirement plans have converted millions of dollars of capital gains into ordinary income.

A StretchIRA trust, on the other hand, does not convert capital gains into ordinary income. If the trust generates capital gains, there is no tax until the gains are distributed to the income beneficiaries, at which time they would be treated as capital gains, not ordinary income.

To qualify as a tax-exempt trust after the plan owner's death, the trust must meet certain rules. Key among these rules is that the income beneficiaries may retain the right to an income stream, not less than five percent per year, from the trust for a period that can last a very long time, but generally not more than about sixty years. Instead of the plan beneficiaries' taking over the retirement plan, and having to withdraw the entire amount over ten years, and pay ordinary income tax on the entire plan balance, the entire plan balance goes into trust, where it stays and can generate income for the beneficiaries. At the end of the trust term, which will be decades – in most cases many decades – after the end of the contributor's life, the balance remaining in the trust can be used to establish a charitable legacy for the contributor.

Asset Protection

In addition to the tax benefits of a StretchIRA trust, because it is a trust, a StretchIRA trust can include a spendthrift clause which under certain circumstances will protect the trust assets from any claims that might be brought against the trust income beneficiaries. This extra benefit comes for free if the trust is properly drafted.

Ability to Provide for Children, Grandchildren

A StretchIRA trust can be structured so that after the plan owner's spouse dies, the contributor's children can receive the income. In most cases, even the plan owner's grandchildren can be in line to receive income. There is no stated maximum possible term for a trust, but the expected life of most StretchIRA trusts would be in the range of fifty to sixty years.

Payouts and Trust Term

The plan owner who names a StretchIRA trust as the beneficiary of a retirement plan can decide who will be eligible to receive payouts from the trust. Usually, if the owner is married, the plan owner's spouse will be named to receive income for life, then their children, and then their grandchildren. But anyone, regardless of relationship, can be named.

In most cases, the owner and/or spouse can also name one or more children, or nieces or nephews (or anyone, really) to be a successor income beneficiary. In some cases, depending on the ages involved, grandchildren can also become beneficiaries after their parents and grandparents are no longer living.

The expected term of most StretchIRA trusts is determined by the length of the lives of the beneficiaries, and by reference to actuarial tables. In the typical case, the expected life of the trust will be 50 to 60 years. At the conclusion of the trust term, the trust assets can be used to fund a legacy charitable endowment, which can be administered by the plan owner's grandchildren or great-grandchildren.

Deferral Option

A properly constructed and properly managed StretchIRA trust can provide a period of tax-free deferral during which no payments are made to the beneficiaries, and instead the assets grow, inside the trust, tax-free.

When this deferral is in place, the trustee maintains a bookkeeping account called an accumulation account. Each year while deferral is occurring, the amount that would have been eligible to be paid, but wasn't, is added to the accumulation account. For example, if a trust could have paid out $50,000 a year but is in deferral mode for five years, after five years there would be $250,000 in the accumulation account. If after five years deferral was no longer desired, this accumulated amount could then be paid, in whole, or in part, in one year or over multiple years. In addition, the annual payment from the trust could be paid on top of the accumulated amount.

Professional Management

StretchIRA trusts should be managed by professionals. The management is frequently split between a trustee who attends to all the trust-specific compliance, accounting, reporting, and tax returns, and an investment manager who handles the investments.

Tax Reporting

A StretchIRA trust is a separate tax-reporting entity. Even though the trust itself is tax exempt, it must file tax returns. These returns may be quite complex, but such complexity does not affect the income beneficiary.

Each income beneficiary will receive a tax form k-1 from the trust. These forms are typically one page of information.

Tax Treatment of Payments

Section 664 provides that a StretchIRA trust keep track of four tiers of income. These tiers, roughly speaking, are 1) ordinary income 2) long-term capital gains 3) tax-exempt income and 4) trust capital.

When a trust earns income, that income goes (in an accounting sense) into the appropriate bucket. When the trust makes a payment to an income beneficiary, the tax law says that those payments are deemed to come first from ordinary income, until that bucket is empty, then from long-term capital gain until that bucket is empty, and so on.

Limitations

The income beneficiaries of a StretchIRA trust do not have access to the trust principal. For example, if a plan distributes $1 million to a trust, the first beneficiary (often a spouse) will have the right to the income payout, usually five percent, for life, and then potentially the lives of one or more children, and even grandchildren. But the trust principal itself does not belong to the beneficiaries.

In other words, after the plan owner dies and the plan pays its assets to the StretchIRA trust, the beneficiaries own the right to a stream of payments from the trust. This stream of payments is a capital asset. There is a secondary market for streams of trust income, and under some circumstances it is possible to sell this right.

Key Decisions

Once you've decided to use a StretchIRA trust, there are only two (relatively) easy decisions to make:

- Do you have a spouse who you want to be a successor income beneficiary?
- Who do you want to be income beneficiaries after you and/or your spouse?

Timing

When you use experienced advisors to create your StretchIRA trust, your trust can be created easily and quickly, in no more than a few days. The trust must be in place when the plan owner dies.

Because of this necessity, Sterling Foundation Management has created a "standby" StretchIRA trust. This standby trust is created, and then put in standby mode, which is extremely economical to maintain. When the plan owner dies, the assets flow directly into the StretchIRA trust, and avoid the SECURE Act death tax.

To learn more about this trust, reach out to us at our email, Stretch@SterlingFoundations.com, and mention this book.

15. Business Owner Trusts

Selling a business is usually a lengthy, involved, and stressful process for the owner.

It can also be fraught with the "hidden" danger of losing a third, or more, of the gain immediately after the sale.

How?

Because the seller failed to plan adequately for the tax cost of selling.

EXAMPLE

Like so many small and medium size business owners, Steve[27] had built a business in California. The business had done well, but Steve felt California was to be doing its best to drive him away. At 62, he had made more money than he figured he'd ever spend, and didn't need to keep working. His kids were adults and living their own lives, and Steve and his wife decided they were going to move to a place they felt more comfortable. They chose Houston.

As is frequently the case with businesses, Steve's business was worth a lot more than he had put into it, and his tax basis, after depreciation, was functionally zero. And because Steve's business was fairly capital in-tensive, Steve had depreciated a lot of heavy equipment over the years. While that depreciation helped to keep his taxes down then, upon sale he would have to realize at least a million dollars of recapture, subject to tax at ordinary rates.

The business was expected to net about $10 million in a sale, and Steve's basis was effectively zero. Steve, like many business owners who have spent a good portion of their lives building a business, was in no mood to share $4 million with the government.

After examining the alternatives, Steve opted for a Business Owner Trust.

BUSINESS OWNER TRUST

A Business Owner Trust is a tax-exempt trust. Contributions of ownership in an appreciated business to such a trust are tax-free, and the trust can then immediately sell the business with no capital gains tax due at the trust level. (C-corporations are on their income the same regardless of who owns them). The trust then can reinvest the entire proceeds into a diversified portfolio. Furthermore, as long as the assets remain in the

---

[27] Names and facts may or may not represent actual people and situations.

trust, there is no tax on income or capital gains realized by the trust. In addition, the contributor of business to a Business Owner Trust will generally receive a tax deduction for at least ten percent of the value of the assets contributed.

Consider an example where Rick sells a business for a $1.5 million gain. Without planning, Rick would face losing 1/3rd of his gain, or half a million dollars, to taxes. But if Rick contributed the $1.5 million value business to a properly structured Business Owner Trust, the trust could immediately sell the business, recognizing the entire $1.5 million. The trust would owe no tax, and so it would have $1.5 million to invest in a diversified portfolio of assets. In addition, Rick could receive an income tax deduction in the year the business was placed into the trust.

To qualify as a tax-exempt trust, the trust must meet certain rules.[28] Key among these rules is the rule that the contributor may retain the right to an income stream, not less than 5% per year, from the trust for a period that can last a very long time, but generally not more than about sixty years. The contributor gives up the right to the trust principal, and keeps the right to the income stream. At the end of the trust term, which will usually be well after the end of the contributor's life, the balance remaining in the trust can be used to establish a charitable legacy for the contributor.

Asset Protection

In addition to the tax benefits of a Business Owner Trust, because it is a trust, a Business Owner Trust can include a spendthrift clause which under certain circumstances will protect the trust assets from any claims that might be brought against the trust income beneficiaries. This extra benefit comes for free if the trust is properly drafted.

Ability to Provide for Children, Grandchildren

A Business Owner Trust can be structured so that after the original contributor, and spouse, die, the contributor's children can receive the income. In some cases, even the contributor's grandchildren can be in line to receive income. There is no stated maximum possible term for a trust, but the expected life of most Business Owner Trusts would be in the range of fifty to sixty years.

Payouts and Trust Term

The business owner who contributes to a Business Owner Trust can decide who is eligible to receive payouts from the trust. Typically, the

---

[28] See IRC section 664.

owner will retain the right to receive payouts, usually 5% of the trust value each year, for life.

The owner's spouse can also be a beneficiary, and in the vast majority of cases the trust can last for at least the longer of the spouses' lives.

In addition, in most cases, the owner and/or spouse can also name one or more children, or nieces or nephews (or anyone, really) to be a successor income beneficiary. In some cases, depending on the ages involved, grandchildren can also become beneficiaries after their parents and grandparents are no longer living.

The expected term of most Business Owner Trusts is determined by the length of the lives of the beneficiaries, and by reference to actuarial tables. In the typical case, the expected life of the trust will be 50 to 60 years. At the conclusion of the trust term, the trust assets can be used to fund a legacy charitable endowment, which can be administered by the owner's grandchildren.

Deferral Option

A properly constructed and properly managed Business Owner Trust can provide a period of tax-free deferral during which no payments are made to the beneficiaries, and instead the assets grow, inside the trust, tax-free.

When this deferral is in place, the trustee maintains a bookkeeping account called an accumulation account. Each year while deferral is occurring, the amount that would have been eligible to be paid, but wasn't, is added to the accumulation account. For example, if a trust could have paid out $50,000 a year but is in deferral mode for five years, after five years there would be $250,000 in the accumulation account. If after five years deferral was no longer desired, this accumulated amount could then be paid, in whole, or in part, in one year or over multiple years. In addition, the annual payment from the trust could be paid on top of the accumulated amount.

Professional Management

Business Owner Trusts should be managed by professionals. The management is frequently split between a trustee who attends to all the trust-specific compliance, accounting, reporting, and tax returns, and an investment manager who handles the investments.

Tax Reporting

A Business Owner Trust is a separate tax-reporting entity. Even though the trust itself is tax exempt, it must file tax returns. These returns might be quite complex, but such complexity does not affect the income beneficiary.

Each income beneficiary will receive a tax form k-1 from the trust. These forms are typically one page of information.

Tax Treatment of Payments

Section 664 provides that a Business Owner Trust keep track of four tiers of income. These tiers are, roughly speaking, 1) ordinary income 2) long-term capital gains 3) tax-exempt income and 4) trust capital.

When a trust earns income, that income goes (in an accounting sense) into the appropriate bucket. When the trust makes a payment to an income beneficiary, the tax law says that those payments are deemed to come first from ordinary income, until that bucket is empty, then from long-term capital gain until that bucket is empty, and so on.

Limitations

The income beneficiaries of a Business Owner Trust do not have access to the trust principal. For example, if an owner contributes $1 million to a trust, that owner will have the right to the income payout, usually 5%, for life, and the life of a spouse, and then potentially the lives of one or more children, and even grandchildren. But the trust principal itself no longer belongs to the owner.

In other words, after the owner contributes a business to the Business Owner Trust, the owner goes from owning the business outright to owning the right to a stream of payments from the trust. This stream of payments is a capital asset. There is a secondary market for streams of trust income, and under some circumstances it is possible to sell this right.

ALTERNATIVES

In most cases of a business sale, there are few good alternatives to a business owner trust, as it minimizes the loss caused by taxes on sale.

"Tax Shelters"

Some sellers consider investments, perhaps things like opportunity zones, oil drilling, or equipment leasing, to generate losses or that otherwise offset the gain of selling a business. Properly structured, these investments are legal and can provide tax benefits. But they are usually also specific investments that may carry risks that it is difficult for the business seller to appreciate.

Few sellers will be happy if they avoid the tax loss, but instead incur an investment loss because they invested in a risky endeavor just to reduce the taxes on the sale of their business.

Basis Step-Up

The first alternative his advisor suggested was that Steve hold the business until his (Steve's) death, so that when he died, his estate would receive a "stepped up basis" and the estate could then sell and not have to pay tax. Steve said he knew that, but as he figures to live for many more years, that's not a solution.

Especially for small and medium sized businesses in which the entrepreneur who built the business is still an important person (the great majority of such businesses), holding till death to get a step up can be a bad idea.

It's a bad idea not because of taxes, but because it is frequently the case that as an entrepreneur ages, especially if he lives to an old age, he slows down and does a less good job of running the business. But even more it is a bad idea because usually the business can be sold more effectively if the person who built it, who knows everything there is to know about it, can be involved in the sale to help make sure that the full value is clear to the buyer.

Incidentally, the use of a Business Owner Trust will usually remove the value of a step-up in basis, because the Trust can sell the business while the business owner is still alive, and not pay the capital gains taxes.

SOME ADVICE: DON'T BE BLINDED BY "THE DEAL"

We have worked with hundreds of owners over the years, and there are some patterns that recur. Most people sell a business only once. And most people naturally tend to think that the main goal in selling a business is to get the most money for their business. That's not wrong, but the selling price, the "headline" price, is not necessarily the only or the best measurement of how good a deal is. And sometimes it can be misleading.

What Are You Getting?

If you are receiving a lump sum of cash, with no contingencies, no warranties, and no potential future liabilities, then the "headline" price is the price. However, this kind of transaction is rare when selling a business. Below are a few examples of bad outcomes when owners have focused too heavily on the headline price. Then, we can look at some real-life examples of when Sterling has made the difference and helped an owner sell their business successfully.

Mr. B. Takes Stock

Mr. B was a brilliant inventor who developed and commercialized a process for DNA replication (or something like that – we never understood the science). He and a partner painstakingly built a successful business over a number of years. Eventually, the partner needed to move on in life, and Mr. B agreed to sell the business. Mr. B was a brilliant scientist, and his partner was a good businessman, but neither had ever sold a business before.

Not knowing any better, without the guidance of a goal-keeper, they hired a blue-chip investment bank, and instructed the bank to get them "the highest price." The bankers were happy to comply, and they did as they had agreed to do. They brought Mr. B and his partner two bona fide offers. One offer was all cash for $50 million, and the other was all stock, for $55 million. Mr. B's partner was in the midst of a divorce, and felt like he needed every dollar he could get. Mr. B, who had never taken a salary greater than $275,000 a year and had no "need" for the extra money, nevertheless, with the encouragement of the investment bank, reached for the extra 10% in the form of stock.

The bankers' motivation was obvious: they got paid as a percentage of the face value of the deal. Mr. B, however, lost sight of his full set of goals. He didn't care only about the face amount of the deal. Mr. B, though he did not articulate it (he only came to the understanding too late), cared about the future stream of cash flows that he could enjoy as a result of the deal. By taking the stock, which he didn't understand and didn't know what to do with, fully, he traded one highly risky asset for another highly risky asset.

You've probably guessed the end of this unhappy story already. Mr. B., having sold his company, became a non-control minority owner in a bigger, but just as risky company. Within a year, the $55 million had shrunk to about $20 million.

Lesson

The lesson from Mr. B's story is clear: when you take stock for the sale of your business, you trade one set of risks for another set. That can work out well, particularly if you understand the risks you are accepting, and you are getting adequately paid to take such risks. There are various ways of determining what "adequately paid" means. Sterling[29] works with

---

[29] Sterling Foundation Management, LLC, the author's employer.

our owner-clients to understand how to think about and value non-cash sales proceeds.

AL-Group Takes a Secured Debenture

The AL-Group business was heavily dependent on the oil industry. When the owner, Al, decided to sell, one of the motivations was to reduce his financial exposure to the concentrated risk of the oil business. Al prided himself on his negotiation skills, and in fact he was a highly skilled negotiator. He let his investment banker know this.

Al sold AL-Group near what turned out to be the top of the market, for a price of $40 million, which represented a rich 8.2 times EBITDA. However, in reaching for the brass ring, the big, bold, brag-worthy headline price of $40 million, Al accepted 80% of the purchase price in the form of a note. The note was a ten-year amortizing, 9.3% debenture, guaranteed by the full faith and credit of the buyer. The buyer assured Al that their goal was to grow the business, they were excited by the growth opportunities, and that's why they were willing to meet Al's high demanded price.

Al felt smug that he was getting not only top dollar for his business, but thought that he was getting the better end of the bargain, because not only was he putting $8 million in his pocket (pre-tax), but he would receive over $410,000 a month for the next ten years. Al's EBITDA in the year prior to the sale had been $4,880,000. Al's investment banker pointed out that the $410,000 monthly payment Al would get, on top of the $8 million up front, was slightly higher than Al's monthly average EBITDA. This observation helped seal the deal.

For the first year or so, everything went smoothly. Then oil prices turned down, and about six months later, so did the business. But Al wasn't worried, and his payments kept arriving, reinforcing in Al's mind his wisdom. After about six months more, however, the buyers informed Al that they would not be able to continue making the full payment each month.

After Al got over his dismay, he contacted his lawyer. They reviewed the deal, and found that, as expected, the buyer would be in default when they missed their first payment. A closer look revealed that the buyer had used a shell company to buy AL-Group. The only real asset was the AL-Group. The terms of the note entitled Al to take back the company, but Al didn't want the company back. With the downturn in the market, EBITDA was down, and multiples were down. In the current market, the business was probably worth only perhaps $18 million, which was less than the remaining $22 million outstanding principal on the note.

After much gnashing of teeth, reviewing his legal options with his lawyer, and crunching many spreadsheets with his accountant, Al decided to renegotiate the note. He accepted interest-only, which meant that his monthly payment dropped to just $175,000 a month.

Lesson

Al's investment bankers, lawyers, and accountants all did the job they were hired to do. Al got a great price for his business. In hindsight, Al – or someone on his team – should have done a better job of understanding the risks in the deal structure that Al, the investment banker and the lawyer worked out. We are not saying that Al made a bad decision. Sometimes you can make a good decision and still have a bad outcome. But Al could have been, and should have been, better informed about the market value of the risk he took when the deal was structured as it was. Sterling can help with such valuations, and as a long-term player, Sterling's incentives are likely to be well aligned with the seller's goals.

Hidden or Implicit Options

In many business transactions, as in both Mr. B's and Al's cases, there are hidden (or not so hidden) "gotchas." Many of these "gotchas" can in fact be identified, and even valued, in advance. Many of these potential problems can be modeled and studied as implicit options. And if they can be modeled as options, an approximate value can often be assigned to them. Sterling has considerable expertise in identifying and valuing certain types of implicit options. One of our principals wrote his doctoral dissertation on implicit options.

EXAMPLES OF SUCCESSFUL SALES

The following are two instances in which Sterling worked closely with a business owner to clarify goals, implement plans to meet those goals, hire an investment banker, sell the business, and (we hope) live happily ever after.

Mr. O's Oil

Mr. O owned an oil production business that managed a large number of oil wells. Mr. O had no clear successor in the business (i.e. no family members, children or key executives willing and able to take over). The older Mr. O got, as with all of us, the closer to the end he came. Not wanting to leave his estate with a business that would suddenly lose value if it lost its guiding hand, Mr. O determined that it was time to think about selling. The price of oil is volatile, and therefore the market value of Mr. O's business was also volatile. An oil production business can be valued in a variety of ways. In the case of O's Oil, the valuation was a combination of sum-of-the-parts and EBITDA multiple. Oil wells are typified by a so-called production curve. In essence, the market expects well production to decline over time. The expected remaining life of a well is thus a major factor in the value of a well. We spent significant time with Mr. O and his team helping to close the valuation gap in advance of the sale.

Sterling helped Mr. O understand the sources of his hesitations about selling, and also to understand the alternatives to selling. With time and attention, he came to understand that the best move for his family, both financially and personally, was to put proper tax, estate and charitable planning in place, and then sell the business.

We worked with Mr. O to help him work through how best to attain his goals throughout the process. We helped find an investment banker who we and Mr. O thought would be a good fit, and helped negotiate the deal between O and the investment banker. Though different deals may call for different arrangements, in this case Mr. O and we agreed, as did the investment banker, that a non-standard fee scale, with a rising percentage above an agreed-on target price, made the most sense. With this incentive structure, it was in the investment bank's best interest to focus, as the more he received from the sale, the more they received. Sterling worked with the lawyers, keeping everyone working towards Mr. O's goals, and not allowing personalities or minor deal points to screw up the deal. Our help made it possible for Mr. O to achieve most of his goals, and walk away with a large cash sum.

Mr. Taylor's Taxes

Mr. Taylor had battled health issues for the final twenty or so years of his life. Every time he got knocked down, he got back up. He owned two prize assets, in two unrelated businesses. The two businesses constituted the bulk of his considerable wealth. His children were actively involved in one of the businesses, and we worked with Taylor to keep that business intact and in the family.

The other business was a food business that had no real sponsorship in Taylor's world. His kids weren't interested in it, and management never seemed to get the bone in its teeth. Taylor had grown tired of the business, and determined to put it up on the block.

Sterling worked closely, from early in the process, to sell Taylor Foods. Thanks to Taylor's cooperation and our careful planning, no one, not Taylor, not his kids, paid income tax on the sale. And when Taylor died, thanks again to good, advance planning which was developed and guided with Sterling closely involved, very little estate tax had to be paid.

This was a near textbook example of the power of good planning. The key ingredients were a client committed to involving a skilled goal keeper, starting the planning process with enough time to do it right, the retention of good advisors, and Taylor's willingness to let Sterling do its job.

16. Installment Sales and Deferred Sales Trusts

A variety of similar strategies called Deferred Sales Trusts are marketed as a strategy designed for individuals and businesses seeking to manage capital gains taxes and maximize the proceeds from the sale of highly appreciated assets.

Deferred Sales Trust is often abbreviated to "DST." DST is a well-known abbreviation for Delaware Statutory Trust. (See Chapter 17). The two types of DSTs are very different, and it is important not to be confused by the similarity of nomenclature.

According to promoters, when you are selling real estate, the deferred sales trust offers an alternative to traditional methods like a 1031 exchange. To understand what a deferred sales trust is supposed to do, and how it is said to work, we need to begin with some background.

INSTALLMENT SALE

Section 453 of the Internal Revenue Code defines an installment sale:

The term "installment sale" means a disposition of property where at least one payment is to be received after the close of the taxable year in which the disposition occurs.

The code continues:

For purposes of this section, the term "installment method" means a method under which the income recognized for any taxable year from a disposition is that proportion of the payments received in that year which the gross profit (realized or to be realized when payment is completed) bears to the total contract price.

Thus, the code recognizes and codifies the conditions under which a seller of property may sell the property, get paid in a series of payments spread over at least two tax years, and defer recognition of part of the gain until that gain is actually received.

In a typical installment sale, the buyer and seller agree on price and terms. The term is at least two years, and the buyer makes a series of scheduled payments. To qualify as an installment sale, each payment must include some element of interest payment. This interest is taxable to the seller as ordinary income. The rest of the payment will likely be treated as long term capital gain and return of basis, if the seller had basis in the property.

There are several main reasons for buyers and sellers to agree to installment sale terms. For a buyer, the reason might be financing. In effect, in an installment sale, the seller provides financing to the buyer, often at better terms and more cheaply than the buyer could obtain financing from a third party.

For the seller, the two main reasons might be 1) to sell a property at a price that the seller believes is otherwise not attainable or 2) to spread the taxable gain out over several years.

Seller's Tax Motivation for Installment Sale

From a seller point of view, there are two main tax consequences to be expected from an installment sale. These are 1) the spreading out of gain and therefore tax on the gain over a period of years and 2) the "conversion" of some of that gain into interest.

Limited Tax Benefits

Usually, the financial benefit to a seller of tax deferral is the fact that the seller has the use of cash that he has not yet paid tax on. In effect, when taxes are deferred, the seller can invest the money that would have been paid in taxes, and keep the gains earned on the money that would have been paid in taxes.

But in an installment sale, the seller does not receive up front the cash to invest. In general, in an installment sale, the taxes become due at the same time the seller receives cash. So, while there is tax deferral, there is also cash receipt deferral, largely defeating the value normally associated with deferral.

A second potentially significant limitation on the tax-saving value to a seller is the fact that a portion of each installment payment (except the first) will be interest. Interest is taxable as ordinary income, which typically is taxable at a higher rate than long term capital gain.

When a seller of real estate sells, usually most or all of the gain is taxable as long-term capital gain. Long term capital gain is usually taxable at lower rates than ordinary income. So, depending on the terms negotiated between buyer and seller, a seller in an installment sale might actually be converting some long-term capital gain into ordinary income. That conversion, of course, is not likely to be tax favorable to a seller. (It may, however, be valuable to a buyer, if the buyer is in a position to deduct interest expense as a business expense.)

Tax Benefit

Given the preceding four paragraphs, you might be wondering, "So, where is the tax benefit to a seller from an installment sale?"

The answer is that the tax benefit is subtle, and may not apply, particularly to larger sales or for high income sellers.

That's because the primary benefit, when there is one, comes from shifting taxable income from a higher bracket to a lower bracket.

Example

Here is a simplified example of how an installment sale could save a seller taxes by moving capital gains from the highest 20% bracket to the 15% bracket. For a married couple, as this is written, the federal 15% long term capital gains tax bracket covers the income interval from (rounded) $100,000 to $600,000. In other words, assuming no other income or deductions, capital gains over $600,000 will be taxed at 20%, and between $100,000 and $600,000 at 15%.

The actual tax rules are significantly more complicated than the following example. The intention of the example is to show how an installment sale could save taxes.

Suppose a couple has a capital gain of $1,000,000, and absolutely no other income or deductions (very unlikely, but helps keep the example from getting too complex).

If the couple sells the property, realizes the $1 million gain in a single calendar year, and receives the entire $1,000,000, they will pay tax on the last $400,000 (the amount of the gain that exceeds $600,000) at a rate of 20%.

If, instead, they break the sale into two equal installments of $500,000 (ignore interest, ignore time value of money, ignore transaction costs, ignore credit risk) spread into two calendar years, the entire $400,000 gain that would have been taxed at 20% will instead be taxed at 15%.

That represents a potential tax saving of 5% of $400,000, or $20,000. Or, looked at differently, the savings is 2% of the total gain. That benefit is certainly not nothing, but it's also not huge.

Credit Risk

In the real world, a seller who sells on an installment basis usually ends up becoming the creditor of the buyer. If the buyer has good credit, that might not be a problem. But selling and accepting a note in partial payment introduces a new element of risk that would not exist if the property were sold for cash.

If the seller is adequately compensated for that risk, then that risk simply becomes another element of the transaction. But if the seller is not adequately compensated, however, the additional risk should be counted as another cost of the installment sale. And if that risk is accepted merely in order to realize an overall tax savings of 2% of the sale proceeds, the potential savings might not be worth the risk.

Market Value of Private Notes

Another important factor that some sellers overlook is that the fair market value of a private note is often significantly less than the face value of the note. For example, suppose that buyer and seller agree on a price of $1 million. If the sale is for cash, the seller receives proceeds with a fair market value of $1 million.

But if the same sale were for $500,000 at closing, and an installment note for the remaining $500,000, the note is likely to have a fair market value of less than $500,000.

There are three main reasons private notes (as opposed to standardized and publicly traded notes like Treasury notes, certain bank Certificates of Deposits, and certain corporate bonds) have lower fair market value than equivalent publicly traded notes. These are credit risk, lack of marketability, and risk of collectability.

These additional risks would generally cause an equivalent private note to bear a much higher interest rate as compared to an investment grade publicly traded note. For example, ASA appraiser Bruce A. Johnson estimated that if a corporate bond yielded 5%, an equivalent private debt instrument would have to yield 12% to 20% to have the same fair market value.[30]

STRUCTURED INSTALLMENT SALE

In the early 2000s, Allstate Insurance was already familiar with the idea of structured settlements. Structured settlements were and are a way of handling large damage claims paid to individuals who, if they were to receive a large lump sum, might mismanage it and end up broke.

Allstate built on their familiarity with the structured settlement market and expanded it to the idea of a structured installment sale.

Allstate realized that the credit risk to a seller would be greatly reduced if a highly rated insurance company, instead of an unknown, unrated buyer, were on the other side of the installment note.

So, the structured installment sale was born.

A structured installment sale works best for small transactions with sellers in low tax brackets. For example, consider a couple in their 50s

---

[30] *How to Value Privately Held Promissory Notes*, Bruce A. Johnson, Today's CPA, September/October 2019, p. 30.

with low income selling a business for a $1,000,000 gain. A lump sum sale would, for that year, throw them into the 15% tax bracket for most of the sale, and the 20% bracket for $400,000 of it. Overall, they would pay about $155,000 of capital gain tax. (This example is oversimplified).

In an idealized (i.e. oversimplified) case, a structured installment sale might allow the seller to spread the gain over, say, 11 years. With interest, the seller might receive (the actual numbers depend on many factors, including interest rates, commissions, and transaction costs) $100,000 a year. Most of that would be capital gain, and much of that capital gain would be taxed in the zero bracket.

As good as this sounds, Allstate found that it was not a sustainable business, and they left the business in around 2010. More recently, another insurance company has taken up the idea and is marketing it heavily.

DEFERRED SALES TRUST

All that background gets us to the idea of a deferred sales trust.

A deferred sales trust (often perhaps misleadingly called a "DST") is supposed to provide the seller with a lump sum of cash. It is built on an installment sale.

There are many versions of deferred sales trusts that purport to provide a panoply of benefits to the seller. However, many are also marketed subject to non-disclosure agreements, making it difficult to evaluate the claims of promoters. Many commentators view the non-disclosure agreement requirement as a red flag, or even a non-starter.

The Deferred Sales Trust, in its various forms, seems to be a legal and financial structure that according to promoters allows the seller of an asset to defer capital gains taxes. The seller transfers ownership of the asset to a third-party trust before the sale. The trust then sells the asset to the buyer, receiving the proceeds of the sale.

Instead of immediately realizing a taxable event, the seller becomes a beneficiary of the trust and receives installment payments over time. These payments are typically structured to provide ongoing income, and capital gains taxes are paid only when payments are received, allowing the seller to spread the tax burden over several years or decades

IRS Crosshairs

Perhaps the most important thing to know is that the IRS has targeted similar structures. Here, in full, is the text of the IRS' Chief

Council Notice CCA_2019103109421213, number 202118016 discussing "monetized installment sales."[31]
Number: 202118016
Release Date: 5/7/2021

From:
Sent: Thursday, October 31, 2019 9:42:12 AM
To:
Cc: Bcc:
Subject: Installment Sale Analysis

This is in response to your request for our analysis regarding "Monetized Installment Sale" transactions. Note that because there are multiple promoters/sub-promoters, there could be variations in the way transactions are structured. Some of the points below might not apply to every transaction. However, there do seem to be common features that make the transactions problematic. And we generally agree that the theory on which promoters base the arrangements is flawed. The general structure raises a number of issues including, but not limited to, the following:

1. No genuine indebtedness. At least one promoter contends that the seller receives the proceeds of an unsecured nonrecourse loan from a lender, but a genuine nonrecourse loan must be secured by collateral. A "borrower" who is not personally liable and has not pledged collateral would have no reason to repay a purported "loan." See Estate of Franklin v. CIR, 544 F.2d 1045 (9th Cir. 1976). Therefore, the loan proceeds would be income.

2. Debt secured by escrow. In one arrangement, the promoter states that the lender can look only to the cash escrow for payment. It appears that, in effect, the cash escrow is security for the loan to taxpayer. If so, taxpayer economically benefits from the cash escrow and should be treated as receiving payment under the "economic benefit" doctrine for purposes of section 453. Compare Reed v. CIR, 723 F.2d 138 (1st Cir. 1983).

3. Debt secured by dealer note. Alternatively, the Monetization Loan to taxpayer is secured by the right to payment from the escrow under the installment note from the dealer. This would result in deemed

---

[31] https://www.irs.gov/pub/irs-wd/202118016.pdf

payment under the pledging rule, under which loan proceeds are treated as payment of the dealer note. Section 453A(d).

4. Section 453(f). The intermediary does not appear to be the true buyer of the asset sold by taxpayer. Under section 453(f), only debt instruments from an "acquirer" can be excluded from the definition of payment and thus not constitute

Perhaps the most important thing to know is that the IRS has targeted similar structures. Here, in full, is the text of the IRS' Chief Council Notice CCA_2019103109421213, number 202118016 2

`payment for purposes of section 453. Debt instruments issued by a party that is not the "acquirer" would be considered payment, requiring recognition of gain.

See Rev. Rul. 77-414, 1977-2 C.B. 299; Rev. Rul. 73-157, 1973-1 C.B. 213; and

Wrenn v. CIR, 67 T.C. 576 (1976) (intermediaries ignored in a back-to-back sale situation).

5. Cash Security. To the extent the installment note from the intermediary to the seller is secured by a cash escrow, taxpayer is treated as receiving payment irrespective of the pledging rule. Treas. Reg. section 15a.453-1(b)(3) ("Receipt of an evidence of indebtedness which is secured directly or indirectly by cash or a cash equivalent . . . will be treated as the receipt of payment.")

6. NSAR 20123401F is distinguishable. The case addressed in the memorandum did not involve an intermediary. Further, loans to a disregarded entity wholly owned by seller were secured by the buyer's installment notes, but the pledging rule of section 453A(d) was not applicable. There is an exception to the pledging rule for sales of farm property, which applied in the case.

Thank you, and please let us know if you have any questions.

BOTTOM LINE

Installment sales can work to the benefit of the right sellers, with the right circumstances, at the right time.

Deferred Sales Trusts, however, according to some observers, take the idea a step too far. Certain versions have attracted the unwanted attention of the IRS, as illustrated in the above reproduced IRS notice.

The bottom line seems to be that deferred sales trusts and similar transactions may carry significant tax and other risks that render them inappropriate for most people.

17. Delaware Statutory Trusts

The term Delaware Statutory Trust, often abbreviated "DST," is used in a variety of ways, some of which may cause confusion.

Delaware Statutory Trust Defined

Technically, a Delaware statutory trust is any trust created to conform to the requirements of the Delaware Statutory Trust Act, 12 Del. C. § 3801 et seq.

Delaware Statutory Trusts in Use

In practice, the vast majority of Delaware statutory trusts in use actually function like real estate partnerships or pooled funds, for the purpose of being the target property in a 1031 exchange.

A 1031 exchange is a sale of real estate, and the prompt replacement of that real estate by new real estate, that qualifies for tax-deferral under Internal Revenue Code section 1031.

Limited Appeal of Delaware Statutory Trusts

Based on our observations of the market, and discussions with a number of market participants, it appears that the majority of investors in Delaware statutory trusts make the investment as part of a 1031 exchange.

This implies that relatively few investors ever invest in a Delaware statutory trust because they believe it is independently an attractive investment.

That may be because of a number of limitations that attach to Delaware statutory trusts compared to other real estate investment vehicles.

For the passive investor in real estate, the overwhelmingly preferred ways are direct real estate ownership, and ownership through a REIT, or real estate investment trust.

REITs

REITs are investment companies that invest almost exclusively in real estate, distribute at least 90% of their annual taxable income directly to shareholders, and unlike standard corporations, are not double taxed. Most REITs are publicly traded, making them liquid on a daily basis, and making it very easy to determine the fair market value of a share in a publicly traded REIT.

For all these reasons, REITs have grown from a tentative beginning in the 1970s to become by far the preferred way for portfolio investors to invest in real estate.

LIMITATIONS OF DSTS

Particularly compared to REITs, Delaware Statutory Trusts are inferior real estate investment vehicles in most ways.

Illiquidity

Delaware statutory trust investments are typically illiquid, for two major reasons. The first reason pertains to the trust itself. A Delaware statutory trust acquires a real estate holding, and then holds that property for a term of years, typically specified. The Delaware statutory trust cannot refinance the property, or sell it, without triggering adverse tax consequences.

There is no liquid secondary market for Delaware statutory trust interests, though in specific instances and specific trusts it may be possible to sell interests before the maturity of the trust.

Long Term

When a Delaware statutory trust is offered, the discussion may focus on the idea that the trust will last for, say, five to seven years. But the documents, such as the private placement memo, may allow the trust to last significantly longer, even fifteen years.

Lack of Control

Investors in Delaware statutory trusts have no say in the investments of the trust, and even if they did it wouldn't make much difference because, as noted above, the trust is designed to just buy and hold whatever real estate it starts with.

Concentration Risk

A major reason some real estate owners sell an appreciated property is to achieve diversification. Unfortunately, most Delaware statutory trusts own a very undiversified portfolio of property. Often, a trust will own only a single property. Depending on what real estate is being exchanged into the Delaware statutory trust by a seller, the seller might actually end up with more risk than before.

Fees

Delaware statutory trusts can come with high up costs, and high ongoing fees. For example, a reasonably typical private placement memorandum for a Delaware statutory trust that was investing in retail space, shows that of $44.5 million raised, only about 87% of that was to go into the property. The remaining 13% was accounted for by fees and costs of various sorts.

The up-front fees include commissions to retail brokers (the people who sell the Delaware statutory trust interest to the clients exchanging their real estate for the Delaware statutory trust interest) of up to 6.5%, a "nonaccountable marketing and due diligence allowance" of up to 1%, and a .5% commission override to an affiliated broker-dealer. There is another up to 1% that will be paid either to a broker-dealer or retained by the sponsor.

In addition, the deal carries a number of other going fees, including an asset management fee of up to 0.4%, a property management fee of 2.81% to 2.9% of the gross rental income of the property, 2% of gains on sale.

If you are looking at an offering document and would like help understanding the deal being offered, contact us by email at DSTfees@SterlingFoundations.com.

BUSTED 1031

Section 1031 is complex, but for real estate sellers looking to complete a 1031 exchange, some of the salient points are that a seller has 45 days after selling the first property to identify the replacement property, and 180 days to complete the purchase of the replacement property.

More often than you might think, a real estate owner sells, intending to enter a 1031 exchange, but is in danger of failing to identify the replacement property within the allowed 45 days.

In such a case, the seller might turn to a Delaware statutory trust as an alternative to paying the capital gains tax. Whether or not that makes sense may depend on the specific facts.

Underlying Property

A Delaware statutory trust cannot be any better than the underlying property. Any investor considering a Delaware statutory trust should look carefully at the underlying property, and make the decision in the same way that investor would make any investment decision.

Often the underlying property is fine, but unlike REITs, Delaware statutory trusts are typically very undiversified, even a single property, and even a single credit risk.

INCOME AND TAXATION OF INCOME

Delaware statutory trusts may sometimes be used because the property owner is not aware that there may be better alternatives, such as a Real Estate Shelter Trust (see Chapter XXX). The other common reason for using a Delaware statutory trust is to rescue an otherwise busted 1031 exchange.

"High Income"

Some Delaware statutory trusts are sold as high-income producing vehicles. It is advisable to look closely at the claims for the amount of income to be distributed. The early year promised distributions might not be sustainable. Here's a simple example of why that can be the case.

Consider the example above, in which only 87% of the investors' capital even went into the property. We'll make some additional simplifying assumptions to illustrate. Let's suppose that the underlying property has a yield of 6% (reasonably high in today's environment).

Because only 87% of the investors' capital is going in, the investors' yield automatically drops to 5.22%, even before ongoing management fees, and similar. Here's the math.

Suppose that investors put up $1,000,000. Of that million, only 87%, or $870,000 goes into the property. At 6%, that $870,000 produces $52,200 of income. That translates into a 5.22% yield on the $1 million value.

Taxation of Delaware Statutory Trust Distributions

The distributions from a Delaware statutory trust are likely to consist mostly of ordinary income. The reason is that real estate rents, lease payments, and mortgage interest, are ordinary income. And except for the sale of the property (which is to be deferred, that's the purpose of the Delaware statutory trust in most cases), there is no other source of income.

In addition, there is likely to be little depreciation to offset the rental income.

Thus, the income that is distributed is in most cases likely to consist mostly of ordinary income, taxable at the highest applicable tax brackets.

With All These Limitations, Why Use a DST?

Delaware Statutory Trust real estate investments are used almost exclusively as replacement property in 1031 exchanges.

For small real estate positions (e.g. perhaps less than $1 million of market value), a seller might want to defer the tax on sale, and be willing to put up with the limitations of a DST to gain that deferral. If the seller dies holding the DST units, the units will generally get a stepped-up basis for the seller's surviving heirs.

Exiting a DST

But short of the seller dying, a Delaware statutory trust is generally not a permanent solution. The typical trust is intended to last for five to seven years. At the end of the trust period, the investor will either have to make additional plans, or pay the tax.

For alternatives to an additional Delaware statutory trust (with its accompanying fees), investors in existing Delaware statutory trusts may wish to consider a Real Estate Diversification Trust.

18. Charitable Remainder Trusts

Enacted as part of the Tax Reform Act of 1969, §664 of the Internal Revenue Code codified the conditions under which a split interest trust can be tax exempt. This section established what came to be known as charitable remainder trusts, often referred to by the acronym "CRT."

A charitable remainder trust is an irrevocable, non-grantor trust that must have both charitable and non-charitable beneficiaries. Under Section 664 of the Internal Revenue Code (IRC), a charitable remainder trust allows a donor to make a deferred charitable donation and receive income during the donor's lifetime or for a specific number of years. The term "charitable remainder trust" derives from the fact that assets remaining in the trust at the end of the trust term, are paid to one or more charitable organizations.

There are two main types of charitable remainder trusts: Charitable Remainder Annuity Trusts (CRATs) and Charitable Remainder Unitrusts (CRUTs).

These trusts are very similar, and differ primarily in how the amount of income paid to the lead (also called income) beneficiaries is determined.

The term "annuity" in a CRAT refers to a fixed dollar amount that is payable each period (usually quarterly or annually) to the income beneficiary. This payment amount is determined when the trust is created, as a percent of the contribution amount. The payment dollar amount remains constant throughout the life of the trust, regardless of the performance of the trust's assets.

The term "unitrust" in "CRUT" means that the trust distributes a stated percentage of the fair market value of its net assets, and that amount is reassessed every year. Thus, the income from a CRUT fluctuates with the value of the underlying assets. This means that the income can rise, or fall.

All CRTs must be irrevocable, meaning that once it is established and funded, the donor cannot alter the key terms of the trust. There are a few specific changes that might be permitted, but for the most part, donors should consider CRTs as unchangeable.

Charitable Remainder Unitrust Types

Charitable remainder unitrusts come in four major varieties. These are:

- Standard Charitable Remainder Unitrust ("S-CRUT" or "SCRUT")
- Net Income Charitable Remainder Unitrust ("NiCrut")

- Net Income with Makeup Charitable Remainder Unitrust ("NimCrut")
- "Flip" Charitable Remainder Unitrust ("FlipCRUT")

A standard Crut pays out the specified percent (5% to 50%) of the beginning asset value each year. It pays out of income if there is, and out of principal if there is not enough income to make the payment.

A NiCrut pays out only its net income each year, up to the stated payout rate. For example, suppose a NiCrut had a payout rate of 5%, and the trust earned 6% in a given year. The payout would be limited to 5%.

A NimCrut is like a NiCrut, but includes a "makeup" provision. For example, suppose a 5% NimCrut earns 4% income in year one. It will pay out the 4%, and the 1% will be accounted for as an amount that can be paid out in a future year. If the following year the NimCrut earns 7% income, the trust will pay out 6% for that year, consisting of the 5% annual payment, plus the 1% that was not paid out in the prior year.

A Flip Crut begins life as a NimCrut, and upon the occurrence of a specified event (e.g. the death of a donor, the sale of an illiquid asset) the trust becomes a standard Crut.

Tax Deferral

One key tax advantage of a CRT is the ability to defer or eliminate capital gains tax on the sale of appreciated capital assets, such as stocks or real estate. When a donor contributes appreciated property to a CRT, the trust can sell the asset without triggering capital gains tax because the CRT is a tax-exempt entity. This enables the trust to reinvest the full proceeds from the sale. With the deferred tax amount available to invest, the trust will generate greater dollar returns (assuming investment returns are positive) as compared to the dollar returns which would be generated, everything else equal, if the tax were paid up front.

This is because if the asset were sold by the donor, a significant fraction (up to a third or more depending on state and local income taxes) would be lost to taxes. With a CRT, the income beneficiaries receive taxable distributions over time. Sometimes this can result in income being taxed at lower marginal rates than if the asset were sold at one time. But the larger benefits usually arise simply from deferral.

The income received by the beneficiaries is subject to taxation under a four-tier system, which dictates the order in which various types of income are distributed and taxed. The first tier includes ordinary income, such as interest, dividends, and rental income. This income is taxed at the beneficiary's regular income tax rate. If the trust does not have sufficient ordinary income to meet its payout obligation, the second tier, capital gains, is tapped. Capital gains are taxed at the applicable capital gains tax rate, which is typically lower than ordinary income tax rates. The third tier includes tax-exempt income, such as interest from municipal bonds. If the trust holds tax-exempt assets, this income is distributed next, providing potential tax-free distributions to beneficiaries. Finally, the fourth tier is a return of principal, which is not taxable but reflects a depletion of the original assets contributed to the trust.

See the following chapter for a more detailed description of the four tier taxation rules.

CRTs must adhere to specific payout requirements to qualify as charitable remainder trusts under the IRC. For both CRATs and CRUTs, the trust must specify annual payout rates to beneficiaries of at least 5% but not more than 50% of the fair market value of the trust's assets.

For CRATs, because the dollar amount is fixed, the payout amount is determined when the trust is funded initially. A donor may not add funds to a CRAT.

A CRUT must also pay out at least 5% of the trust's value, but the percentage is based on the fair market value of the trust's net assets as revalued each year. This distinction makes CRUTs more flexible, especially when the trust's assets are expected to appreciate over time. However, the possibility of lower payouts exists if the assets underperform. Additionally, CRUTs allow for additional contributions to the trust, whereas CRATs do not permit further funding once established.

To qualify for tax-exempt status under §664, the present value of the remainder must be at least 10% of the value of the assets at the time of contribution. This 10% value is calculated according to rules laid out in the IRS code and regulations.

This "10% remainder rule" ensures that the charity will receive a significant gift at the end of the trust's term. The 10% rule imposes limits on the permissible rate of payment (even within the 5% to 50% rules), and/or the permissible duration (term) of the trust.

If the payout rate or term of the trust is too high relative to the expected performance of the trust's assets, the trust will fail to meet this requirement, disqualifying it from CRT status. In practice, the calculation of the remainder interest involves the use of actuarial tables and IRS discount rates, which are updated periodically and reflect the current interest rate environment.

Another much-mentioned benefit of a CRT is the charitable income tax deduction available to the donor in the year the trust is funded. The amount of the deduction is based on the present value of the charitable remainder, calculated using the IRS's Section 7520 rate, which approximates the expected rate of return for the trust's assets.

Everything else equal, the lower the Section 7520 rate, the higher the value of the remainder interest, and thus, the greater the charitable deduction. This deduction is subject to limitations based on the donor's adjusted gross income (AGI), with the ability to carry forward unused deductions for up to five years. The deduction provides immediate tax benefit, and provides another inducement for grantors to support charity.

Estate Taxes

CRTs are often used as estate planning tools to reduce estate tax liability. By transferring assets to a CRT, donors may effectively remove the contributed assets from their taxable estates. This will, in general, be the case when the trust lasts no longer than the life of the donor, or in the case of a husband and wife, no longer than the life of the survivor.

When the death of the husband or wife ends the trust, the assets pass to charity at the end of the trust's term, and thus the assets qualify for the estate tax charitable deduction, effectively removing the assets from the taxable estate, and thereby decreasing estate tax exposure. For high-net-worth individuals facing significant estate tax burdens, and who like the idea of a significant portion of their wealth passing to charity upon their deaths, a CRT can be a useful strategy for preserving wealth, providing income, and benefiting a charitable cause.

Asset Protection

Asset protection is another potential benefit of using a CRT. Because the CRT is irrevocable, assets transferred to the trust are generally shielded from creditors, as they are no longer considered the donor's property. However, if a CRT is created with the intent to defraud creditors, it may be subject to scrutiny under fraudulent transfer laws. Therefore, while a CRT can offer significant asset protection benefits, it must be established in good faith and not as a means to evade existing creditor claims. Income distributions to beneficiaries may in general still be subject to creditor claims depending on the nature of the creditors and the applicable state laws.

The management of a CRT requires careful consideration of investment strategies, tax planning, and compliance with the relevant legal and tax regulations. The trustee of a CRT has fiduciary responsibilities to both the income beneficiaries and the charitable remainder beneficiary. The trustee, or an investment manager delegated by the trustee, must prudently invest the trust's assets to generate sufficient income while also preserving enough principal to meet the charitable remainder requirement. The selection of investments is particularly important in a CRAT, where the fixed payout can erode the trust's assets if returns are inadequate. In a CRUT, the annual revaluation of assets provides some flexibility, but poor investment performance can still reduce the income available to beneficiaries and the remainder for charity.

Trustees must also ensure compliance with the various private foundation rules (generally §4940 et seq.) that apply to CRTs. These include prohibitions on self-dealing, which restrict transactions between the trust and disqualified persons such as the donor, trustee, or their family members. CRTs may also be subject to restrictions on excess business holdings, limiting the percentage of ownership the trust can have in a business enterprise. Trustees should avoid making "jeopardizing investments" that could endanger the trust's assets. CRTs must avoid engaging in taxable expenditures, such as lobbying or political activities. Violations of these rules can result in excise taxes or the loss of the trust's tax-exempt status, which could have significant negative consequences for the trustees, the beneficiaries and the charitable organization.

At the end of the CRT's term, the remaining assets are distributed to the designated charitable organization or organizations. If the actual remainder exceeds the projected value calculated at the inception of the trust, the charity benefits from the additional funds. Conversely, if the trust's performance has been weaker than expected, the charity may receive less than initially projected. The flexibility of the CRT structure allows donors to support a wide variety of charitable organizations, including public charities, private foundations, and donor-advised funds. Donors may specify multiple charities as remainder beneficiaries, or they may designate contingent charitable beneficiaries in case their primary choice no longer exists when the trust terminates.

The termination of a CRT can occur in a variety of ways. Most commonly, the trust ends upon the death of the income beneficiaries or at the conclusion of a specified term, which cannot exceed 20 years. Alternatively, the trust may be terminated early if the beneficiary chooses to donate the income interest to the charity before the trust's term ends. In some cases, a CRT may terminate prematurely if the assets within the trust are exhausted before the payout period concludes, although this outcome is rare with proper management. Upon termination, the charity receives the trust's remainder, fulfilling the donor's philanthropic objectives.

19. Four-Tier Accounting System in IRC Section 664

Section 664 of the Internal Revenue Code includes the rules for income paid from trusts that are tax exempt under the section. These rules are the so-called four-tier accounting system.

This system lays out the basic rules for how distributions to the taxable beneficiaries of a charitable remainder trust are taxed.

The Four Tiers

When a qualified §664 trust makes a distribution to a lead beneficiary, that distribution must be characterized for tax purposes using a tiered system. The code describes the tiers as follows:[32]

Amounts distributed [to a lead beneficiary] shall be considered as having the following characteristics in the hands of a beneficiary to whom is paid the annuity described in subsection (d)(1)(A) or the payment described in subsection (d)(2)(A):

(1) First, as amounts of income (other than gains, and amounts treated as gains, from the sale or other disposition of capital assets) includible in gross income to the extent of such income of the trust for the year and such undistributed income of the trust for prior years;
(2) Second, as a capital gain to the extent of the capital gain of the trust for the year and the undistributed capital gain of the trust for prior years;
(3) Third, as other income to the extent of such income of the trust for the year and such undistributed income of the trust for prior years; and
(4) Fourth, as a distribution of trust corpus.

For purposes of this section, the trust shall determine the amount of its undistributed capital gain on a cumulative net basis.

"WORST-IN, FIRST-OUT"

The basic rule-of-thumb for understanding the taxation of distributions from a §664 trust is "worst-in, first-out."

---

[32] IRC §664(b)

The "worst" refers to the highest rate of tax. So, for example, ordinary income is taxed at the highest marginal rates. Long term capital gains are taxed at lower marginal rates. Tax-exempt income[33] (in most cases) will be the third tier, and the fourth tier, the "least worst" type of distribution, is return of principal (which may also be called corpus or basis).

Tier 1: Ordinary Income

The most common forms of ordinary income in a §664 trust will generally include interest, dividends, rents, and other forms of income that would normally be taxed at ordinary income tax rates if received by an individual.

Note that some types of ordinary income, such as many forms of business income, cannot or should not be earned in a §664 trust because such income might constitute "unrelated business income." See below for a discussion of unrelated business income.

Each trust must keep track of all four categories. Distributions must be made in the order, tier 1 to tier 4.

So, for example, as long as a trust has any tier 1 income on its books, that tier 1 income will be considered to be distributed when cash is distributed.

We provide examples below.

Tier 2: Capital Gains

The majority of §664 trusts are funded with appreciated capital assets. Typically, the trust then sells such assets, recognizing long term capital gains. Those capital gains go into the "tier 2" income account.

Tier 3: Tax-Exempt Income

Tier 3 income is tax-exempt income. In typical cases, a trust is unlikely to ever be in position to distribute tax-exempt income.

If a trust is funded with a low-basis capital asset, and the trust sells the asset, that trust will have the entire amount of the capital gain in the tier 2 account.

For example, suppose a grantor owns $1 million of stock with a basis of $100,000, and contributes it to a §664 trust. When the trust sells the stock, the trust puts (for accounting purposes, there is no separate physical account) the $900,000 gain into the tier 2 account, and the $100,000 of basis into the tier 4 account.

---

[33] Exceptions may include muni bonds purchased at a discount, muni bonds that pay interest subject to the alternative minimum tax, the fact that certain "tax-exempt" income can push recipients into higher tax brackets for Medicare and/or cause their social security benefits to be taxed, or the fact that some muni-bonds are issued as taxable bonds.

Suppose that the trust has a payout rate of 5%, and further suppose that the entire $1 million is invested into tax-exempt bonds that yield exactly 5%. And just for simplicity, assume that the fair market value of the bond portfolio remains at exactly $1 million.

In the first year, the trust will earn $50,000 of tax exempt, tier 3, income. However, the distribution will be deemed to come from the $900,000 of tier 2 income. In the second year the same thing will happen.

In this example, the trust will earn $50,000 of tier 3, tax-exempt, income each year, but will distribute $50,000 of tier 2 (long term capital gain) income for as long as there is income remaining in the tier 2 account.

By our assumptions, it will take 18 years to distribute all the tier 2 income.

Only after that, in year 19, will the distributions be considered to come from tier 3, tax-exempt, income.

As you can see, the other likely way a trust can get to the point where it will distribute tax-exempt income is when the trust is initially funded with cash or high-basis assets.

Tier 4: Corpus, Basis, or Return of Principal

The code refers to tier 4 as "corpus." Other names for the same concept are basis, or trust principal. This tier accounts for the original contributions to the trust, or other receipts that are not considered income for tax purposes. Distributions from tier 4 will not have tax consequences to the recipient because they are not taxable.[34] Distributions from this tier are not taxable to the beneficiary.

Example

Suppose, as above, that a grantor owns $1 million of stock, with a basis of $100,000. He contributes the stock to a qualified §664 trust, and the trust sells it. The trust has a payout rate of 5%. The trust will have $900,000 in tier 2 income, and $100,000 in tier 4. It will have zero in each of the other categories.

Suppose that the trust investment manager invests the $800,000 into the S&P 500, and $200,000 into taxable bonds. Further suppose that the only income from the S&P 500 investment is 2% dividends, and the only income from the bonds is interest at 5%.

The trust's income from stocks is $16,000 (i.e. 2% of $800,000), which goes into tier 2. The income from bonds is $10,000 (5% of $200,000), which goes into tier 1.

---

[34] Given the complexity of the US income tax, it cannot be said with certainty that a tier 4 distribution could never have a tax consequence.

After one year, the trust distributes 5% of $1 million, or $50,000. The distributions come out as follows:

Tier	Beginning Balance	Income	Distribution	Ending Balance
1	0	10,000	10,000	0
2	900,000	16,000	40,000	876,000
3	0	0	0	0
4	100,000	0	0	100,000

20. Charitable Lead Annuity Trusts (CLATs)

A Charitable Lead Annuity Trust (CLAT) is a split-interest irrevocable trust, structured to provide fixed annuity payments to one or more charitable organizations for a predetermined term, after which the remainder interest reverts to non-charitable beneficiaries, typically family members. The primary appeal of a CLAT lies in its ability to achieve charitable giving objectives while enabling the transfer of assets to heirs at a reduced gift or estate tax cost by leveraging the charitable deduction under the Internal Revenue Code (IRC) if the trust assets generate a return greater than the §7520 rate used to value the gift.

The 7520 rate is an IRS-published interest rate, issued monthly under Section 7520 of the Internal Revenue Code. The rate is derived from 120% of the applicable federal mid-term rate (AFR), which is tied to the average interest rates on U.S. Treasury securities with maturities ranging between 3 and 9 years.

To establish a CLAT, the grantor transfers assets into the trust, which is designed to pay a fixed annuity—a fixed dollar amount[35]—to the charitable beneficiary for a set period. The structure is governed by the rules under IRC §2055(e).

The valuation of the charitable interest, for purposes of determining the allowable charitable deduction and the taxable gift of the remainder interest, is dictated by the present value of the annuity stream, calculated using the §7520 rate—the assumed rate of return set by the IRS based on the Applicable Federal Rate (AFR) for the month the trust is funded. This actuarial valuation is central to both the charitable deduction available (if applicable) and the gift tax consequences. The lower the §7520 rate, the higher the present value of the charitable interest, reducing the value of the remainder interest that will eventually pass to non-charitable beneficiaries.

For gift and estate tax planning purposes, the grantor's goal is often to create a structure where the appreciation of the trust assets exceeds the §7520 rate. If this strategy succeeds, it allows wealth to pass to heirs free of additional gift or estate tax at the end of the trust's term. If successful, the excess appreciation benefits the remainder beneficiaries without further transfer tax, making CLATs particularly attractive when funded with assets expected to appreciate significantly during the trust term, such

---

[35] There is such a thing as a charitable lead unitrust, but they are very rarely used.

as closely-held business interests or publicly traded securities with high growth potential.

Grantor CLAT

In a grantor CLAT, the grantor retains certain powers or interests that cause the trust's income to be taxed to the grantor under IRC §§671-679. The principal benefit of a grantor CLAT is the ability to claim an immediate charitable income tax deduction for the present value of the annuity payments to the charity, computed at the inception of the trust under §170(f)(2)(B). However, the downside is that the grantor remains responsible for the income tax on any trust income, even though the annuity payments are made to the charity. The full deduction is recaptured if the trust terminates prematurely or the grantor relinquishes grantor status before the term ends.

Non-Grantor CLAT

A non-grantor CLAT is primarily an estate planning tool. It does not confer an immediate charitable deduction to the grantor but instead allows the trust itself to take charitable deductions under IRC §642(c) for the amounts paid to charity. The trust's income is taxed to the trust itself, subject to the rules applicable to complex trusts. In this structure, no immediate income tax deduction is available to the grantor, but there is no ongoing tax burden to the grantor on the trust's income during the term.

A critical technical aspect of CLAT administration is ensuring the fixed annuity payment complies with IRS rules. The annuity must be paid at least annually and cannot fluctuate based on the trust's actual performance during the term. Failure to meet these requirements could disqualify the trust as a valid CLAT, jeopardizing the charitable deduction and gift tax treatment. Additionally, trustees must navigate the trust's liquidity carefully. If trust assets do not generate sufficient income to meet the annuity obligation, principal must be used, which could deplete the corpus and diminish the remainder interest.

Another strategic consideration in CLAT planning is the term of the trust. The trust can be structured to last for a term of years or for the life of one or more individuals. In practice, selecting a fixed term of years often allows for more precise control over the trust's financial and tax outcomes. The actuarial value of the remainder interest passed to heirs at the end of the trust term is calculated by subtracting the present value of the annuity stream from the initial trust value, and a longer trust term generally increases the value of the charitable interest, thus reducing the taxable remainder.

From a valuation perspective, the initial funding of the CLAT with assets such as marketable securities provide a straightforward calculation of the trust's fair market value. However, when illiquid assets, such as real estate or private equity, are used, the trustee must obtain a qualified appraisal at the time of funding, as required under IRC §2031 and the corresponding regulations. Proper valuation is critical not only for determining the charitable deduction but also for establishing the gift tax liability associated with the remainder interest.

The remainder beneficiaries of a CLAT often benefit from the appreciation of trust assets during the charitable term, provided the trust's returns outpace the AFR used to calculate the charitable deduction. For example, if the trust is funded with $1 million, the §7520 rate is 4%, and the annual annuity is $50,000, the remainder interest could pass to the beneficiaries with minimal additional tax if the trust assets grow at a rate higher than 4%. This dynamic allows significant wealth transfer with reduced gift tax consequences, which is a key reason CLATs are often used in high-net-worth estate planning.

The mechanics of calculating the annuity payments and the remainder interest, as well as ensuring compliance with both federal tax rules and fiduciary obligations, make CLATs a sophisticated tool for charitable giving and estate planning. Given the complex interactions between trust law and the tax code, both at the federal and state levels, the administration of a CLAT requires careful attention to investment strategy, tax compliance, and charitable goals. Trustees have a fiduciary duty to manage the trust's assets prudently under the Uniform Prudent Investor Act, balancing the need to meet the annuity obligations with preserving sufficient corpus for remainder beneficiaries.

While the CLAT itself is not a tax-exempt trust, CLATs may be subject to the private foundation rules under IRC §§4940-4946 if the charitable beneficiary is a private foundation, which may impose additional excise taxes and reporting requirements on the trust. Trustees must avoid jeopardizing the trust's tax-exempt status or triggering penalties under the excess business holdings rules or the jeopardizing investments restrictions.

21. Charitable Trust Funding Rules

WHAT KINDS OF PROPERTY MAY BE CONTRIBUTED TO A CHARITABLE TRUST

The types of property that may be contributed to a charitable trust are diverse, but the deductibility and tax treatment of the contribution depend on the nature of the property and the manner in which it is used by the trust. IRC §170(c) permits the deduction of contributions made to qualified organizations, which includes charitable trusts that meet the requirements of IRC §501(c)(3) and related Treasury Regulations. However, the characterization of the property as real, tangible personal, or intangible, as well as its intended use, directly impacts the donor's tax benefits.

Real Property

Real property is a legal category of property that refers to land, buildings, structures, fixtures and generally includes things like mineral rights. Real property is in the United States pretty much synonymous with real estate.

Contributions of real property to charity are typically eligible for a deduction equal to the fair market value (FMV) of the property, provided the donor relinquishes all ownership and control, as required under IRC §170(f)(3), and provided that the property has been owned for at least the required period for long term capital gain treatment. In the United States, the current required holding period is one year.[36]

Any restrictions on the property, such as conservation easements under IRC §170(h), will in general affect the fair market value of the property for tax purposes. In addition, certain restrictions such as recognized conservation easements, may qualify for tax deductions if they are granted in perpetuity and serve a qualified conservation purpose. When a property is held subject to easement (even if the easement is not a qualified conservation easement), the easement will in general reduce the FMV because the easement represents a portion of the property's value that belongs to someone other than the property owner.

---

[36] In case you're wondering what happens in the case of a leap year, it appears that the required holding period gets extended by one day, 366 instead of 365, see Treas. Reg. §1.421-2(b)(1)(ii).)

Real estate is commonly contributed to a variety of charitable organizations and owners are eligible for income tax deductions based on the fair market value of the property contributed.

Restrictions on Accepting Real Estate

Note that not all trusts or organizations will accept contributions of real property. There may be several reasons for this, which will vary by case and by institution. Among them are: general policy, concern over potential liabilities, inability or unwillingness to manage or dispose of property, concern of the salability of the property, and concern of the cost of managing and/or disposing of the property.

Tangible Personal Property

The category tangible personal property, refers to physical things, such as artwork, vehicles, or equipment, that are not real property. In general, tangible personal property may also be contributed to a charitable trust. However, under IRC §170(e)(1)(B), the deduction for such property is limited to the lesser of its fair market value or the donor's adjusted basis if the property's use by the charity is unrelated to its exempt purposes. For example, if a donor contributes artwork to a trust that sells it for fundraising rather than using it for educational or cultural purposes, the deduction may be limited to the donor's basis.

Intangible Property

Intangible property, including stocks, bonds, and other securities, is frequently contributed to charitable trusts due to its liquidity and ease of valuation. IRC §170(e)(1)(A) specifies that contributions of appreciated securities held for more than one year generally qualify for a deduction equal to fair market value without recognizing the capital gain. This benefit, discussed further in the context of avoiding capital gains realization, is a primary advantage of using charitable trusts for such contributions.

Partial Interests

Partial interests in property are generally disallowed as deductible contributions under IRC §170(f)(3)(A). However, exceptions exist for certain trust structures, such as charitable remainder trusts and charitable lead trusts, where partial interests such as income streams or remainder interests are explicitly permitted under IRC §664 and IRC §170(f)(2). These vehicles allow donors to retain a defined benefit while transferring the remainder or income interest to the charitable trust.

Another exception to the prohibition on deductions for partial interests is IRC section 170(f)(3)(B)(i), which permits a deduction for the "contribution of a remainder interest in a personal residence or farm."

DEDUCTION RULES FOR CONTRIBUTIONS TO CHARITABLE TRUSTS

The calculation of deductions for contributions to charitable trusts is governed by IRC §170, which sets forth rules regarding the valuation, substantiation, and limitations applicable to such contributions. The primary determinant of the deduction amount is the fair market value of the property, as substantiated by a qualified appraisal in accordance with Treasury Regulation §1.170A-13(c) for non-cash contributions exceeding $5,000. The appraisal must be conducted by an independent appraiser, and failure to obtain or report such an appraisal can lead to disallowance of the deduction under §170(f)(11).

What to Look for in an Appraisal

A qualified appraisal is obtained from a qualified appraiser. A qualified appraiser is defined as follows. "For purposes of section 170(f)(11) and § 1.170A-16(d)(1)(ii) and (e)(1)(ii), the term qualified appraiser means an individual with verifiable education and experience in valuing the type of property for which the appraisal is performed, as described in paragraphs (b)(2) through (4) of this section."

Timing

An appraisal must be made in a timely manner. That means the appraisal cannot be for a time more than 60 days prior to the date of the contribution. If the appraisal is done after the contribution (usually the better course of action, though some people want an appraisal before the contribution if they are unsure of the approximate value), the appraisal should be as of the date of the contribution, and made no later than the due date of the tax return (including extensions) for which the appraisal is being used.

Report

A good appraiser will produce a report that satisfies all the requirements as commonly expected in practice. To a layman, an appraisal report may appear to contain a great deal of information not obviously relevant to the case at hand.

For most people, the only real concern with the report is that it be done correctly in a timely manner. And, of course, most people are interested in the value finally arrived at.

Selected Deduction Rules

You can claim a deduction for the fair market value for contributions of appreciated property, such as securities or real estate, only if the property has been held for more than one year and is considered a long-term capital asset under IRC §1221. If the property has been held for less than one year, the deduction is limited to the lesser of fair market value or the donor's adjusted basis, reflecting its short-term status as an ordinary income property under IRC §170(e)(1)(A).

Adjusted basis is not necessarily the same as purchase price. For example, in the case of investment real estate, the basis will typically be reduced by depreciation each year, and increased by capital expenditures. It is generally advisable to consult with a knowledgeable professional, such as a CPA, if there is material doubt regarding the basis.

Special rules apply to contributions of certain types of property, such as inventory or property subject to depreciation recapture under IRC §1245 and §1250. In these cases, the deduction is limited to the donor's adjusted basis to account for potential ordinary income treatment. For property subject to restrictions or encumbrances, the deduction may be reduced proportionally under IRC §170(f)(3)(B).

As with many things in the code, IRC §1245 and §1250 have their complexities. For the most part, 1245 property can be thought of as tangible personal property (in a real estate context, things like furniture, carpeting, and decorative fixtures). Section 1250 property is real property, which generally means the land and building including all the structural parts of the building.

Personal Limitations

Additionally, percentage limitations apply to the total deductions a taxpayer can claim in a given year. Under IRC §170(b), deductions are limited to 30% or 50% of the taxpayer's adjusted gross income (AGI), depending on the type of property contributed and the classification of the charitable organization. Excess contributions can generally be carried forward for up to five subsequent tax years under IRC §170(d).

For individual taxpayers

In 2023 and until the rules change, an individual or couple can deduct a maximum of 60% of Adjusted Gross Income (AGI).

The only way to qualify for that 60% of Adjusted Gross Income limit is to contribute only non-capital gain property (think cash) only to public charities.

The 50% Limit

Otherwise, 50% of Adjusted Gross Income is the maximum that can be deducted.

There are several ways to reach the 50% deduction limit. Two of the most common ways follow. An individual could contribute:

Method 1

30% of Adjusted Gross Income in the form of cash to a private foundation

Plus

20% of Adjusted Gross Income in the form of cash to a public charity

Or

Method 2

20% of Adjusted Gross Income in the form of appreciated publicly traded securities to a private foundation,

Plus

30% of Adjusted Gross Income in the form of cash to a public charity

The 30% Limit

Thirty percent of Adjusted Gross Income is the maximum that can be deducted for contributions only to private foundations. For individuals contributing to private foundations, the 30% can be comprised of up to 20% in the form of publicly traded stock, with an additional 10% in cash or other property whose contribution value is based on basis, not fair market value.

C-CORP RULES

Charitable deductions by C-corporations are generally limited to 10% of taxable income.

Pass-Through Rules

The rules for passthroughs, such as most partnerships and LLCs, do not apply separately to the entity. Rather, the entity, an LLC for example, that makes a charitable contribution, will for tax purposes pass the deduction to the members, usually on a pro-rate basis. Each member will then be subject to the individual limitations

A 100% Exception

There is one type of entity that can deduct up to 100% of its taxable income each year. That type of entity is a qualified charitable lead trust. Charitable lead trusts are typically used in the context of estate planning for large, taxable estates. On relatively rare occasions, charitable lead trusts are used for income tax planning. The effective use of charitable lead trusts requires considerable thought and analysis.

AVOIDANCE OF CAPITAL GAINS REALIZATION UPON CONTRIBUTION

Contributions of appreciated capital gain property to qualifying charitable trusts enable the contributor to avoid realizing the capital gains on the property, even when the property is subsequently sold.

When appreciated property is sold outright, the owner typically recognizes capital gain under IRC §1001, triggering a tax liability on the difference between the sales price and the asset's adjusted basis. However, contributing such property to a qualified tax-exempt charitable trust allows the donor to defer or entirely avoid the recognition of gain.

Fair Market Value Deduction

For contributions of long-term capital assets, such as securities or real property, IRC §170(e)(1)(A) permits a deduction based on fair market value without requiring the donor to recognize the inherent gain. This benefit is contingent upon the property being transferred to the charitable trust before any binding agreement to sell the property is made.

Anticipatory Assignment of Income

One of the concepts involved is the so-called "anticipatory assignment of income" or simply "assignment of income" doctrine. Under this taxation concept, the government claims the right to tax income "to those who earn or otherwise create the right to receive it." This was established by the Supreme Court in Helvering v. Horst, 311 U.S. 112, 119 (1940).

In a separate case, Estate of Hoensheid v. Commissioner the tax court wrote "donors must bear at least some risk at the time of contribution that the sale will not close."

The General Rule

When a property owner contributes appreciated property to any qualified charitable organization, the grantor usually has the dual desires to a) obtain an income tax deduction and b) avoid realization of the gain when the property is later sold.

Following a case called Palmer v. Commissioner, the IRS issued Rev. Rul. 78-197, adopting a "bright-line" test. The following is a quotation from the ruling:

[T]he Service concluded that it will treat the proceeds of a redemption of stock under facts similar to those in Palmer as income to the donor only if the donee is legally bound or can be compelled by the corporation to surrender the shares for redemption. The Tax Court has characterized the "legally bound" standard in Rev. Rul. 78-197 as a "bright line" test for determining if a contribution of stock to a charity followed by a redemption of that stock from that charity should be respected in form or recharacterized as a redemption of the stock from the donor followed by a contribution of the proceeds by the donor to the charity.

In all cases, careful adherence to IRC requirements and proper structuring of the contribution are essential to avoid unintended recognition of capital gain. To qualify for a deduction and avoid recognition, the transfer of property to the trust must be irrevocable, there must be no legally binding obligation to sell, and the deduction must be properly substantiated. Other rules may apply in certain situations.

VALUATION AND SUBSTANTIATION RULES

To receive a deduction, a donor must substantiate the fair market value of the property at the time of the contribution to determine the allowable deduction. For non-cash contributions exceeding $5,000, a qualified appraisal is mandatory. The appraisal must comply with Treasury Regulation §1.170A-13(c), ensuring that the valuation reflects a bona fide market analysis performed by an independent and credentialed appraiser. In general, the valuation must be made no more than 60 days prior to the contribution, and before the tax return on which the contribution is being claimed is due.

Importantly, this means that a contribution can be made, and then the valuation completed by a qualified appraiser sometime after the contribution. In most cases, a form 8283 will also be required when the contributor files tax returns.

BARGAIN SALE RULES

Yet another potential issue is the issue called bargain sale. Despite the name that suggests a sale is involved, a bargain sale can occur even when there is no sale.

The bargain sale rules, codified under IRC §1011(b), derive their name from the fact that they do apply when property is sold to a charitable organization for less than fair market value. Such transactions are treated as part sale and part charitable contribution. While the portion of the transaction considered a charitable contribution may qualify for a deduction, the sale portion triggers recognition of gain, which can result in unintended tax consequences.

Debt

The bargain sale rules can also be triggered by the contribution of property that is subject to debt. The value of the contribution is the fair market value, less the debt. However, in addition, the contributor will also be considered to have received income to the extent of the debt.

In addition, the debt causes the basis to be pro-rated, with only part of the basis being allocated to reduce the gain.

The rules are complex, and each case should be considered individually.

Example

Consider a scenario in which a property with a fair market value of $1,000,000 and an outstanding mortgage of $400,000 is gifted to a charity. The donor's basis in the property is $600,000. The debt is treated as being transferred to the charity, and the donor is treated as though he received the amount of the debt as income.

The donor must then base his basis between the "sale" portion (represented by the mortgage) and the "gift" portion (the remaining equity).

The basis allocation is found by multiplying the basis by the ratio of the mortgage to the fair market value. The basis is $600,000. The ratio of the mortgage to the fair market value is 40% (i.e. $400,000 / $1,000,000). Forty percent of the donor's basis is $240,000.

The donor is then deemed to have sold the property for $400,000, against which he can apply the basis of $240,000. This results in a taxable gain of $160,000.

But we're not done yet. The donor can also claim a charitable contribution deduction. This deduction is equal to the difference between the fair market value of the property and the total realized by the charity, which is $600,000. The $600,000 is what is left to the charity after selling the property for the fair market value of $1 million, and paying off the debt of $400,000. This deduction may be subject to limits on charitable contributions.

If this seems complicated, that's because it is. Professional advice is strongly recommended.

DOCUMENTATION AND REPORTING REQUIREMENTS

Charitable contributions must be property reported and substantiated, or the donor is at risk of losing the deduction. For non-cash contributions exceeding $5,000, donors must obtain a qualified appraisal that meets the standards outlined in Treasury Regulation

§1.170A-13(c). The appraisal must include detailed information about the property, the methodology used to determine fair market value, and the qualifications of the appraiser.

Donors must attach Form 8283 to their tax returns and obtain a contemporaneous written acknowledgment from the charitable trust. This acknowledgment must describe the contributed property and confirm that no goods or services were received in exchange for the contribution.

Failure to meet these requirements can result in the disallowance of the deduction, penalties, and potential scrutiny. Donors are strongly advised to engage qualified professionals to assist with the valuation, documentation, and reporting process to ensure compliance and protect their tax benefits.

CONCLUSION

The contribution of property to a charitable trust can offer significant tax advantages when executed correctly. Adhering to the rules governing tax deductibility, timing of transfers, and trust structuring is essential to avoiding pitfalls such as the assignment of income doctrine and the bargain sale provisions. Proper planning, meticulous attention to detail, and compliance with reporting requirements are critical to achieving a successful outcome. Donors would be well advised to work with competent professionals to navigate the complexities, avoid potential pitfalls, and to successfully achieve their objectives.

22. Spousal Lifetime Access Trusts

As of this writing, the scheduled lifetime estate tax exemption is scheduled to be $15 million per person, indexed for inflation. For most people, the estate tax is not likely to bite. But for a significant number of high net worth families, the limit presents a dilemma.

The dilemma is that many of these families who have estates that will likely be taxable are not comfortable giving away a large part of their wealth.

"What if we need it?" is the common fear.

Spousal Lifetime Access Trusts (SLATs) may be part of the answer. The other part, discussed below, is *Asset Protection Trusts*.

By establishing "his and hers" SLATs, couples can use their combined lifetime gift tax exemptions, avoid estate taxes on the assets when they die, and maintain access to trust assets should they need those assets.

UNDERSTANDING SPOUSAL LIFETIME ACCESS TRUSTS (SLATS)

A Spousal Lifetime Access Trust (SLAT) is an irrevocable trust created by one spouse (the grantor) for the benefit of the other spouse (the beneficiary). The trust is designed to remove assets from the grantor's estate, thereby reducing potential estate taxes, while still providing indirect access to the trust assets through the beneficiary spouse.

Key features of a SLAT include:

- **Irrevocability:** Once established, the trust cannot be modified or revoked, ensuring that the assets are removed from the grantor's estate.
- **Lifetime Gifts:** The grantor makes lifetime gifts to the trust, utilizing his or her gift tax exemption.
- **Spousal Access:** The beneficiary spouse has access to trust distributions, providing an indirect benefit to the grantor.

THE CONCEPT OF NON-RECIPROCAL "HIS AND HERS" SLATS

Non-reciprocal "his and hers" SLATs involve each spouse establishing a separate SLAT for the benefit of the other. The trusts must not be identical, and they cannot be "reciprocal." This strategy allows both spouses to create trusts that provide for each other, thereby addressing the fear of not having enough.

The main difference between a SLAT and a standard estate tax planning trust is that the SLAT allows the non-granting spouse to have access to trust assets under some conditions, and yet that access does not bring the trust assets back into the taxable estate of the couple.

A SLAT will typically be set up to take advantage of both estate/gift tax exemption and Generation Skipping Tax exemptions. As such, each spouse can use his or her lifetime gift and GST exemption, effectively removing those assets from the estate tax system "forever."

If creditor protection is a concern, the SLATs can be drafted to protect the assets in trust from future creditors and divorce settlements, providing financial security. (Attempts to shield assets from existing creditors may be considered fraudulent conveyances, or otherwise subject to voiding.)

SETTING UP "HIS AND HERS" SLATS

The process of establishing "his and hers" SLATs requires planning and coordination. Whether these steps are performed by the investors themselves, or by their advisors, the key steps include:

1. **Determine Objectives:** Investors should clearly define their estate planning goals, including tax reduction, asset protection, and providing for each other and future generations.
2. **Identify Assets:** Choose which assets to transfer to each SLAT. It's important to consider the type of assets, their appreciation potential, and the impact on the overall estate plan.
3. **Draft Trust Documents:** Work with an appropriate professional to draft the trust documents. Each trust should have distinct terms to avoid reciprocal trust issues, which can negate the intended tax benefits.
4. **Fund the Trusts:** Transfer the chosen assets into each trust. This process must be handled carefully to ensure compliance with tax laws and avoid potential pitfalls.
5. **Manage the Trusts:** Appoint a trustee to manage the trust assets. The trustee has a fiduciary duty to act in the best interests of the beneficiaries.

RECIPROCAL TRUST DOCTRINE

One of the critical considerations when establishing "his and hers" SLATs is avoiding the reciprocal trust doctrine. This doctrine, which appears to have been created by the courts (instead of a legislature),[37] can allow the IRS to disregard the trusts if they are deemed to be too similar. In such a case, the IRS may deny the validity of the gifts, deeming the assets to remain in the estate of the grantor.

The attorney who drafts the trusts is likely to have his or her own (or the firm's) way of making the trusts different, so that the reciprocal doctrine does not apply. Among these approaches are to vary the terms of the trusts with respect to (for example) distribution rules, beneficiaries, trustees, and assets. Another approach is to separate the creation and funding of the trusts by sufficient time, though there is no clear guidance.

ASSET PROTECTION AND THE USE OF A DISTRIBUTION TRUSTEE

Grantors concerned about asset protection might want to use multiple trustees in different roles. For example, a grantor might have a trustee for general purposes, a separate trustee for investments, and a third trustee whose only task is to decide whether, when, and in what amounts to make distributions.

AVOIDING THE BASIS-STEP-UP TRADEOFF TRAP

Many couples own assets that have appreciated. One common strategy is to plan to hold such assets until one or both of the couple dies, so that the heirs can benefit from a stepped-up basis.

The drawback of this strategy is that in order to receive a stepped-up basis, the asset must remain in the taxable estate.

A solution that is compatible with a SLAT strategy is to fund the SLAT with the lead interest in an Asset Diversification Trust

ASSET DIVERSIFICATION TRUST

An Asset Diversification Trust is a tax-exempt trust. The grantor and typically the grantor's spouse, children, and grandchildren, are

---

[37] See, e.g., U.S. Court of Appeals for the Second Circuit - 109 F.2d 99 (2d Cir. 1940) January 22, 1940, and later United States v. Estate of Grace, 395 U.S. 316 (1969)

beneficiaries of the trust. Because the trust is tax-exempt, appreciated property can be contributed to the trust. When the appreciated property (e.g. stock, real estate, crypto, a business, partnership units, private investments, or other capital gain assets) is sold in the trust, there is no capital gains tax because the trust is tax-exempt. Thus, the basis step-up becomes irrelevant.

ASSET DIVERSIFICATION TRUST + SLAT = BEST OF ALL WORLDS?

The grantors' interest in the Asset Diversification Trust can be used to fund the SLAT. The grantors of an Asset Diversification Trust own the right to receive income from the trust. That right is itself a capital asset. It is called the "lead" interest or the "income" interest in the Asset Diversification Trust.

That capital asset can be used to fund the SLAT.

Using the lead interest in an Asset Diversification Trust to fund a SLAT can be the perfect solution for a couple who want to:
1. Avoid capital gains on an appreciated asset
2. Take advantage of the lifetime estate tax exemption before it sunsets
3. Retain the ability to access the assets they're getting out of their estate

HOW TO IMPLEMENT

The powerful benefits of the marriage of SLATs with Asset Protection Trusts comes with specialized planning. You will probably want to use the services of an estate planning specialist for the SLATs, and a separate Asset Diversification Trust specialist for the Asset Diversification Trust.

Sterling is the leading provider of turnkey Asset Diversification Trusts, and a pioneer in the combining of the two kinds of trusts to produce the amazing combination of benefits the marriage of SLATs with Asset Diversification Trusts provides to couples.

23. Qualified Terminable Interest Property (QTIP)

QTIP is an acronym for Qualified Terminable Interest Property. A QTIP trust is similar to the "A" trust in an A/B estate plan. The QTIP trust is typically less flexible than the "A" trust commonly used.

In the common A/B structuring, the assets and income in the A trust (also called marital trust) are reachable by the surviving spouse. But in a QTIP trust, the survivor has more limited access to, and dispositive power over, the trust assets. The failure to give these powers to the survivor could disqualify the trust from eligibility for the marital deduction. If the trust did not qualify for the marital deduction, the assets in the trust would potentially be subject to gift/estate tax. However, the tax code permits an election for the marital deduction for a qualified QTIP trust (hence the "Q" in QTIP), and with this election the assets are not taxable at the death of the first spouse.

Contrast to Standard "A" Trust

In the standard A trust, the survivor can access principal, and typically has a power of appointment. The power of appointment allows the surviving spouse to decide who (perhaps among a group of specified people, called a 'limited power of appointment' if that's how the trust reads) can receive the assets after the survivor dies.

Structure

Typically, when a grantor establishes a QTIP trust, he transfers assets into the trust, naming his wife as the income beneficiary for life.

Before you worry that the writing makes a sexist assumption, recognize that of course, it could be the wife as grantor and the husband as life beneficiary, but this is far less common. The dominant reasons it is less common are demographic and actuarial. In the United States, among older couples the husband is on average 4 to 5 years older than the wife. In addition, at age 60, the life expectancy of a male is 22 years, while for a woman it is 65 years. These two facts explain why on average, men die years before their wives.

Second Marriages

In cases of second marriages, it is common for a grantor (we'll assume the husband for discussion purposes, though it could be a wife) to have children from a first marriage to whom that grantor wishes to leave the bulk of his estate. But he also wants to provide for his second wife for her life should he predecease her.

The QTIP structure, because it allows the first dying spouse (the husband by assumption) to control who gets the assets (typically his children from a first marriage) is most frequently seen in second marriage situations.

Requirements

There are a number of restrictive requirements that a QTIP must satisfy to qualify as a QTIP. Among the more significant of these are:

- A QTIP trust must provide that the surviving spouse is entitled to all of the income from the trust, payable at least annually.
- No person other than the surviving spouse may receive distributions from the trust during her lifetime.
- The income must be paid to the surviving spouse, not less than annually.
- The surviving spouse must be a US citizen.
- The surviving spouse must have the right to demand that the trustee convert non-income producing assets into income-producing assets.
- The surviving spouse's right to the income must be unconditional, meaning that, for example, the right remains even if the survivor remarries.
- Trust principal is generally not available to the survivor.

One of the primary advantages of a QTIP trust is its ability to qualify for the unlimited marital deduction. This means that assets transferred to the trust are not subject to estate tax at the first spouse's death, regardless of the value of the assets. The estate tax is instead deferred until the death of the surviving spouse. This deferral can be particularly valuable in situations where the first spouse to die has a large estate that would otherwise be subject to significant estate taxes, because it may allow the surviving spouse to implement tax-mitigating planning that was not done during the life of the first spouse.

Control Freak Danger

In the course of our business lives, we have seen a surprising number of situations in which the husband generated a large taxable estate, yet refused to implement any effective estate-tax mitigation approaches. This may be the case, for example, where a husband is a "control freak" and simply refuses to give up what he perceives as control.

After the husband dies, the surviving wife, being less of a control freak, is willing to actually engage in estate planning. However, if the control freak has locked the assets in an irrevocable trust, the surviving spouse may have limited ability to implement effective planning.

FLEXIBILITY

The flexibility to make a partial QTIP election allows for post-mortem estate planning, as the executor can determine the optimal amount to elect based on the circumstances at the time of the first spouse's death.

Consider an example in which John, who has children from a previous marriage, wants to provide for his current wife, Sarah, but also ensure that his children ultimately inherit his assets. John creates a QTIP trust in his will, funding it with $10 million of assets. Upon John's death, the trust provides Sarah with all the income generated by the trust assets for her lifetime. John's executor makes the QTIP election on the estate tax return, allowing the entire $10 million to qualify for the marital deduction. When Sarah eventually passes away, the remaining trust assets will be distributed to John's children as he originally intended.

Partial QTIP Election

The assets in a QTIP are not subjected to estate tax until the death of the surviving spouse. Thus, the easy default is to elect to put all the assets in the QTIP trust. But there could be situations in which the executor would optimize the family's situation by choosing to apply the QTIP election to only a portion of the assets.

For example, suppose that a portion of the assets is in a business, and the value of the business is believed to be depressed at the time of the first spouse's death. The executor might determine that, in his view, the best time to pay the estate tax on those assets is now, because he thinks those assets are likely to appreciate sharply between now and the death of the surviving spouse. Especially if there is enough cash or liquid assets in the estate to pay the tax, that might be seen as a lower risk, higher reward strategy. He might then allocate to the QTIP only the non-business assets, and the liquid assets that remain after allowing for the payment of the estate tax on the value of the business.

Invasions of Principal

In some cases, QTIP trusts may include provisions for principal invasions for the benefit of the surviving spouse. These provisions typically limit distributions to an ascertainable standard related to health, education, maintenance, and support. While such provisions can provide additional security for the surviving spouse, they must be carefully drafted and administered to preserve the trust's qualification for the marital deduction.

Another consideration in QTIP trust planning is the potential for disclaimer planning. A well-drafted estate plan might include provisions that allow the surviving spouse to disclaim all or a portion of the assets intended for a QTIP trust. These disclaimed assets could then pass to a credit shelter trust or directly to children, potentially optimizing the overall estate tax situation based on circumstances at the time of the first spouse's death.

Basis Step-Up

Because the assets in a QTIP are includable in the survivor's estate, the assets in a QTIP trust receive a step-up in basis at the death of the surviving spouse, just as they would if they were owned outright by the surviving spouse. However, the effective capital gains tax rates, even in the highest tax states, are still lower than the federal estate tax rate, so it is not cost effective to pay estate tax merely to avoid capital gains tax.

INFLEXIBILITY

QTIP trusts are irrevocable, and involve some degrees of inflexibility that can be a disadvantage if circumstances change. QTIP trusts generally cannot be modified or terminated without potentially severe tax consequences. This in flexibility underscores the importance of careful planning and consideration before implementing a QTIP trust strategy.

The process of unwinding a QTIP involves consideration of many issues, both legal and tax, and the advice of a qualified professional is highly recommended.

Tradeoffs

In practice, the use of QTIP trusts often involves balancing competing interests. The grantor must weigh the desire to provide for his spouse against the goal of preserving assets for children or other beneficiaries. The trustee, in turn, must manage trust assets in a way that generates sufficient income for the surviving spouse while also preserving principal for the remainder beneficiaries. This balancing act can sometimes lead to tension or even litigation, particularly in blended family situations.

To illustrate the practical application of a QTIP trust, consider a scenario where Robert, a successful business owner with two children from his first marriage, is married to Linda, who has one child from a previous relationship. Robert wants to ensure that Linda is provided for after his death, but he also wants his business interests to ultimately pass to his children. Robert establishes a QTIP trust in his will, funding it with his business interests valued at $20 million. Upon Robert's death, the trust provides Linda with all the income generated by the business. Robert's executor makes the QTIP election, deferring any estate tax. Linda receives income from the business for her lifetime, but she cannot sell or transfer the business interests. Upon Linda's death, the business interests pass to Robert's children as he intended.

In this example, Robert has in effect prohibited the sale of the business, even if a great, above market offer were to come along. He has done so, presumably, because he wants to ensure that the business itself, and not its market value, passes to his kids.

This is merely an example of one of the many tradeoffs that might be involved when a grantor contemplates the use of a QTIP trust.

CONCLUSION

QTIPs are used primarily in cases of large estates, and more frequently in the case of second marriages. The law involved, and the analysis of competing interests and potential scenarios, while important in any estate planning context, may be particularly complex in cases where QTIPs may be appropriate. Hence, potential grantors are advised to seek competent advice before implementing any such planning.

24.   Marital and Bypass Trusts

You might sometimes hear the term, or encounter, a "Bypass Trust." This kind of trust is also sometimes known as a "credit shelter trust" or "B trust." These are typically associated with "Marital Trusts" or "A" trusts.

Each is not so much a special kind of trust, but rather a specialized use of a trust, typically used by married couples to minimize federal estate taxes. Such trusts were much more common when the estate tax exemptions were lower, before 2001. Prior to 2001, the estate tax exemption was only $675,000, meaning that the estate tax ensnared tens of thousands of people. Today, with the estate tax exemption at around $15 million per person, fewer couples feel the need to plan around it, and as a result we see fewer Bypass trusts.

WHAT IS A BYPASS TRUST?

The purpose of a Bypass trust is to maximize the use of each spouse's estate tax exemption.

The typical use is, after the first spouse dies, two trusts are funded, often called an "A" trust and a "B" trust. The "B" trust is the bypass trust. This is usually accomplished via each spouse's will, by including the provision in both spouses' wills that upon the event of the first death, that spouse will create and fund a bypass trust up to the amount of the exemption.

Marital Trust

The "A" trust is also called a "marital trust." The "A" trust is solely for the benefit of the surviving spouse while that surviving spouse is alive. As such, the assets in the A trust are not subject to estate tax at the death of the first spouse because they qualify for the marital exemption (unless the surviving spouse is not a US citizen).

The "B" or Bypass trust is typically funded up to the limit of the decedent's remaining lifetime exemption. These assets therefore pass to the subsequent generations without estate tax and the trust ensures that the deceased spouse's exemption is fully utilized, preventing it from being wasted as it would be if all assets were simply transferred to the surviving spouse under the unlimited marital deduction. The assets placed in the bypass trust are not included in the surviving spouse's taxable estate, thereby reducing potential estate taxes upon the survivor's death.

Irrevocable

The bypass trust must be irrevocable upon its creation, meaning its terms cannot be altered by the surviving spouse. Nevertheless, the surviving spouse may retain certain valuable powers over the bypass trust. These powers may include a so-called power of appointment.

Power of Appointment

A power of appointment can give the surviving spouse the right to funds in the bypass trust for specific, designated purposes. Common examples of such purposes are healthcare, and education or education-related expenses. There may also be the right for the surviving spouse to designate who (a "general" power of appointment) or who among a named group of individuals (a "limited" power of appointment) can get trust assets after the survivor's death.

Typically, the surviving spouse can receive income generated by the bypass trust during their lifetime but cannot access the principal. And typically, the surviving spouse is not required to take all the income from the Bypass trust, leaving the possibility of passing more to the heirs.

EXAMPLE

Consider a couple with a combined estate valued at $30 million. By setting up both a bypass and a marital trust, they can protect up to $30 million from federal estate taxes based on current exemption limits. If one spouse dies first, $15 million can be transferred into the bypass trust—fully utilizing that spouse's exemption—while the remaining $15 million goes into a marital trust. The surviving spouse receives income from both trusts but does not have control over the principal in the bypass trust.

Establishing a marital bypass trust involves certain complexities and costs. Drafting these trusts typically requires legal expertise to ensure compliance with tax laws and to address specific family circumstances. Additionally, ongoing administrative duties such as record-keeping and tax filings are necessary to maintain compliance and manage distributions. These responsibilities might necessitate hiring professional trustees or advisors.

Limitations

There are limitations inherent in using a bypass trust. Since it is irrevocable upon creation, any changes in family dynamics or financial circumstances cannot alter its terms. For instance, if unforeseen expenses arise for the surviving spouse or beneficiaries, accessing additional funds from the bypass trust may not be possible without violating its terms.

With today's estate tax exemption of about $14 million per person, such concerns do not apply in the vast majority of situations in which a bypass trust might be indicated.

State Death Taxes

As of 2025, 17 states, plus the District of Columbia, have some sort of death tax on their books. People who live in or might otherwise be subject to (e.g. they own property in one of these states) death taxes in one of these states should, in addition to their federal estate planning, consider the state death taxes. The use of an A/B trust plan can help, but readers are advised to retain competent local counsel to advise on the complex and frequently changing area of state death taxes.

"Portability"

Portability is a concept that permits a surviving spouse to add to the survivor's lifetime estate tax exemption any unused amount of the deceased spouse's estate and gift tax exemption. For example, assuming that the individual exemption is $14 million, neither spouse has used any exemption, and the husband dies using $6 million, then the survivor would have her own $14 million, plus the husband's unused $8 million, for a total of $22 million.

Most states with death taxes do not allow portability. This may further complicate the estate planning process.

However, most of the states with death taxes do not tax gifts, meaning that there may be low or no-tax ways to avoid the death taxes in those states with planning.

CONCLUSION

The A/B, or marital/bypass structure is much less frequently seen than before 2001, largely because fewer estates are subject to the estate tax. For those estates that are, or may likely be, subject to estate taxes, the dual trust structure can still be a standard part of the estate planning toolkit to minimize taxes while taking care of the surviving spouse, and the heirs.

25. Grantor Retained Annuity Trusts (GRATs)

A grantor retained annuity trust (GRAT) is a specialized use of an irrevocable grantor trust, for the purpose of moving future growth in asset value out of a taxable estate, typically using little or no estate tax exemption.

Note that a GRAT is generally not used to remove existing value from an estate, but rather only appreciation. In our experience, many commentators seem to miss this fact.

Grantor retained annuity trusts are usually referred to as GRATs, and that is the terminology we will use in this section.

HOW A GRAT WORKS

A GRAT works as follows. A grantor creates a GRAT for a specified period of time, such as five years. The grantor then funds the trust with an asset (or assets). The grantor retains an annuity from the trust, which must be paid to the grantor every year. During the annuity period, the grantor is the only current beneficiary of the trust. At the conclusion of the annuity period, which is the conclusion of the trust, if the grantor is still living, the value remaining in the GRAT passes to the grantor's heirs (the people, or it could be another trust) named in the GRAT.

The estate planning benefit is that at the successful conclusion of a GRAT, the remaining assets pass out of the grantor's estate with no further estate or gift tax.

Annuity

As the term GRAT implies, the grantor of a GRAT retains an annuity for the term of the trust. That annuity must be defined as a specified stream of cash flows. These cash flows must be paid to the grantor whether or not the GRAT earns income sufficient to cover the cash flows.

The GRAT may distribute non-cash assets back to the grantor to satisfy required annuity payments. When non-cash assets are used to make the annuity payments, the assets used must be valued appropriately as of the date the annuity payment is made.

In the case of hard-to-value assets, it is highly advisable to have a qualified appraisal made for the purpose of valuing the GRAT payment, rather than relying on another appraisal that may have been done at a different time for a different purpose. For example, See IRS CCA 202152018 regarding a case in which the IRS reached the conclusion that the appraisal used was "outdated" and "did not take into account all the facts and circumstances." The IRS determined that the retained annuity was not a qualified annuity interest, defeating the grantor's intended planning purpose.

Income Tax

To the extent that the GRAT does earn income, the grantor will generally be responsible for paying any income tax due on that income. This stems from the fact that the GRAT is a grantor trust. Following the general grantor trust rules, the grantor's payment of the income taxes on the trust's income is not considered to be an additional contribution to the trust. All else held equal, the grantor's paying the income taxes on the trust's income acts like an additional, non-taxed, gift to the ultimate GRAT beneficiaries.

Term

GRATs must be trusts that last for a specified term of years. For a GRAT to succeed, the grantor must survive past the term of the trust. With an older grantor, this consideration should be taken into account.

There is no specific limit on the maximum term of a GRAT, a GRAT must be for at least two years. Obama twice proposed legislation to require a minimum term of ten years, and that was reintroduced, but did not pass, during the Biden administration.

Most GRATs seem to be for periods of between two and ten years.

Rate of Return

The assets in a GRAT must over the course of the trust's life earn an average in excess of the so-called Section 7520 rate in effect for the month that the GRAT was created. If the GRAT fails to achieve this rate of return, at the end of the GRAT, all the assets in the GRAT revert to the grantor, and there is no gift.

The 7520 rate is defined as follows:

Pursuant to Internal Revenue Code 7520, the interest rate for a particular month is the rate that is 120 percent of the applicable federal midterm rate (compounded annually) for the month in which the valuation date falls. That rate is then rounded to the nearest two-tenths of one percent.[38]

---

[38] https://www.irs.gov/businesses/small-businesses-self-employed/section-7520-interest-rates-for-prior-years#:~:text=Pursuant%20to%20Internal%20Revenue%20Code,two%2Dtenths%20of%20one%20percent.

The applicable federal midterm rate is calculated using the yields on US Treasury securities with maturities between 3 and 9 years. As a result, the 7520 rate follows the yield on US Treasuries quite closely.

Single Contribution Only

A grantor is allowed to make only a single contribution to a particular GRAT. That contribution must be at the inception of the GRAT. If the grantor (or anyone else) were to make another contribution in the future, that future contribution would disqualify the GRAT. The result would be that the grantor is considered to have made a current gift, which not only defeats the purpose of the GRAT but is likely a significantly worse outcome than if no GRAT had been attempted. Thus, it is necessary to pay strict attention in the management of the GRAT, to assure that no additional gifts to the GRAT occur.

Gift or Estate Tax

At the end of the trust term, if the grantor has survived, and if the assets have returned at least the required 7520 rate, and if the other requirements (e.g. all the payments have been made and properly valued) have all been satisfied, the assets remaining in the trust will pass to the heirs without further tax. The amount of gift tax exemption will be determined using the annuity payment schedule and the 7520 rate that was in effect when the trust was funded.

Whether there is any tax will depend on the correctly calculated value of the gift, and the amount of exemption that the grantor has remaining.

Example

A grantor contributes $10 million to a GRAT in a month when the section 7520 rate is 3.4%. The grantor retains an annuity of $1,000,000 for 10 years. At the end of 10 years, the remainder will be distributed to a trust for the grantor's heirs. The annuity value is calculated to be $8,358,700. Therefore, the remainder interest is $10 million less the annuity, or $1,641,300.

This remainder value will be the gift value if the GRAT succeeds.

If the assets appreciate at exactly 3.4%, the grantor will receive a stream of 10 payments of $1,000,000, and the beneficiaries will receive $2,292,968 at the end of the 10-year term.

The planning technique in this case would be not really different from simply having made the taxable gift at the beginning of the period.

For GRATs to really be worthwhile, the assets have to appreciate significantly faster than the 7520 rate.

Zeroed Out GRAT

Careful attention to the calculation of the remainder interest shows that it is possible to have GRAT terms that result in the value of the remainder interest, for tax purposes, to be zero.

Here is a simple example. Consider a two-year GRAT, funded with $10 million. Assume that the 7520 rate is 4%. If the annual payment back to the grantor is set at $5,301, 961 the calculated value of the gift for tax purposes will be just zero. If the trust in fact earns 4%, the remainder value will also be just about zero.

But suppose the trust earns the long run average return on the stock market of 10%. The gift amount for tax purposes is still the same zero. In two years, however, the value that passes from the GRAT to its beneficiaries would be $965,000

If you're handy with a spreadsheet, it is not difficult to build a model to make these calculations. If you'd like a sample model, please reach out to us at GRAT@SterlingFoundations.com. The lawyers want us to note that any such information or calculators we supply are for educational purposes only and should not be relied upon for legal or tax purposes.

GRAT Payout Rate Can Change

A GRAT annuity payment does not need to be strictly fixed. If planned in advance, the annuity payment can be increased each year, up to 20% annually. For more on this, see Sec. 25.2702-3(b)(1) of the IRS regulations.

A grantor might want to use an increasing payout rate if, for some reason, he believes that the growth of the asset in the GRAT will be greater in the earlier years of the GRAT than in the later years.

Timing

The annuity payments must be made within 105 days of each anniversary of the creation of the trust. This number, 105, happens to be the number of the day of April 15 (in a non-leap year) when measured from the first of the year. This also corresponds to the wording in the IRS regulations about the required timing of GRAT annuity payments. Section 25.2702-3(b)(4) reads, in part:

An annuity amount payable based on the anniversary date of the creation of the trust must be paid no later than 105 days after the anniversary date. An annuity amount payable based on the taxable year of the trust may be paid after the close of the taxable year, provided the payment is made no later than the date by which the trustee is required to file the Federal income tax return of the trust for the taxable year (without regard to extensions).

Note also that annuity payments are not permitted to be accelerated, prepaid or "commuted," which are all pretty much the same thing.

Discounted Property

Because a GRAT achieves its tax saving purpose only to the extent that the actual returns on the trust's assets exceed the 7520 rate, the use of discounted assets to fund a GRAT is a common technique. Using discounted assets can help increase the probability that the trust's assets, over the term of the trust, will exceed the 7520 rate.

Consider a minority share in a closely held company. Because such a share may lack marketability (there are few if any buyers) and lack control (because the votes are not sufficient to exert any meaningful control over the operation of the company), a qualified appraiser may (and usually will) apply a discount for the lack of marketability and control.

For example, assume that the closely held company distributes its net income every year. A grantor owns 25% of the company. The company generates $1 million a year, and the grantor's share of that is $250,000. A qualified appraiser might value the entire company at, say, $10 million. Twenty-five percent of that $10 million is $2.5 million. But after applying the discounts for lack of control and marketability, the appraiser values the minority 25% interest at $2 million.

The cash flow of $250,000 on $2 million is a 12.5% return. Thus, this 25% minority interest might be a good choice of property with which to fund a GRAT.

Number of GRATs

A grantor may form multiple GRATs, provided that each one is formed and operated correctly. Some people use a series of "rolling" GRATs, with the idea being that even if they don't all exceed the required 7520 rate of return, because markets tend to have good years and bad years, that over time, some of the GRATs will hit good "up" years and will have sizable returns that get significant value out of the grantor's estate without any significant tax impact.

Option Analysis

The attentive reader may observe that a GRAT has several characteristics of a call option. In the Black-Scholes intellectual framework, a call option's value depends on five factors: the price of the underlying asset, the strike price, the risk-free interest rate, the term of the option, and the dividend payment on the underlying.

This framework maps fairly well to the use of a GRAT. In a GRAT context, the underlying asset is whatever the grantor selects to place in the GRAT. The term is the term of the GRAT. The strike price is the future value of the initial assets, grown for the term of the trust at the 7520 rate, the annuity payment corresponds to the dividend on the underlying stock. The risk-free rate does not enter explicitly into the GRAT calculation (though the 7520 rate is based on the yields on mid-term US Treasury securities, which many people consider to be "risk free.").

The full option analysis is beyond the scope of this chapter, but readers can contact us at GRAToptions@SterlingFoundations.com to learn more.

26. Qualified Personal Residence Trust

A Qualified Personal Residence Trust (QPRT) is a specialized trust designed to help individuals reduce their taxable estates in a way that leverages limited lifetime gift tax exemption. A QPRT can be used for a primary or a secondary residence.

By placing a residence in a QPRT, the homeowner retains the right to live in the property for a predetermined period (known as the "retained interest" period), after which ownership of the property passes to designated beneficiaries, often family members.

At the time the property is contributed to the QPRT, only the future value (determined by reference to IRS tables and regulations) is considered to be a taxable gift. Thus, if the grantor survives the period of the trust, this strategy can significantly reduce estate taxes.

The two main benefits of a QPRT result from the dual consequences of this current gift of a future interest. These benefits are 1) as noted, the taxable value of the gift is reduced because the gift is of a future interest, and the present value of that future interest is less than the current value of the home as a whole; and 2) any future appreciation in the value of the home is outside of the grantor's estate. This second feature is also known as a "freeze."

How Does a QPRT Work?

A QPRT is an irrevocable trust that is specifically designed to hold a personal residence. To set up a QPRT, the homeowner transfers the deed of the residence into the trust. The grantor (the person setting up the trust) specifies a set term during which he or she (or a couple) will continue to live in the home and maintain the property, paying related expenses like taxes, insurance, and maintenance costs. This retained right to use the property reduces the value of the gift for tax purposes.

Survivorship

A QPRT must have a specified term, typically a number of years selected to provide the desired discount to the current value of the house. The term should also be selected with the life expectancy of the grantor in mind. For the QPRT to succeed in removing the house from the grantor's estate, the grantor must survive the period of the QPRT.

Provided that the grantor survives the trust term, when the trust term ends, ownership of the property passes to the beneficiaries, often the grantor's children, at the locked-in, reduced valuation.

Rental Period

At that point, the grantor can either move out of the home or pay fair market rent to the beneficiaries to continue residing in the house. The latter option does not allow the grantor to stay in the property, and can also further reduce the taxable estate.

If the QPRT is structured as a grantor trust, the rental payments will not be considered taxable income to the trust. The rental payments will be removed from the grantor's estate. Thus, if making rental payments will not be a burden on the grantor, the rental period can be considered an ongoing benefit of the trust for the grantor's remaining lifetime. However, if the grantor cannot comfortably make the rental payments, the QPRT may not be a good fit. If a grantor fails to make required QPRT rental payments, the house may be brought back into the grantor's taxable estate.

STRATEGIC USES OF QPRTS

Reducing Estate Taxes

The primary strategic use of a QPRT is to reduce estate taxes. By transferring a residence into the trust while retaining the right to live in it for a set number of years, the value of the home at the time of the transfer is discounted based on the grantor's retained interest. This discount means that a potentially substantial asset can be gifted at a much lower valuation, removing it from the taxable estate.

Asset Appreciation Control

Personal residences in the US have, on average, appreciated at slightly greater than the inflation rate over the last century or so. Inflation has averaged about 3.5% since Roosevelt defaulted on the US definition of the dollar in terms of gold. At that rate, the value of a house would double in just 20 years. Those 20 years are close to the life expectancy of a 65-year-old.

A QPRT allows the grantor to freeze the value of the residence at the time of transfer, meaning any future appreciation in the value of the property will not be included in the grantor's taxable estate.

For example, suppose that a 65-year-old owns a home worth $1 million today. That owner creates a 10-year QPRT, and funds it with the home. The gift amount will be approximately $500,000. A gift tax return will need to be filed.

If the grantor lives 20 years, and the home doubles in value, that entire $2 million will be excluded from the grantor's estate.

Protection from Creditors

Once a residence is placed in a QPRT, it is no longer owned by the grantor, potentially providing a layer of protection from potential creditors. This makes QPRTs a potentially attractive option for those concerned about liability risks and asset protection, ensuring that the home is preserved for future generations.

CONSIDERATIONS AND LIMITATIONS

While QPRTs offer significant advantages, there are important considerations and potential drawbacks to be aware of. One of the primary challenges is that the trust must be irrevocable. Once the residence is transferred into the QPRT, the grantor cannot reclaim ownership outside the trust's terms. This lack of flexibility requires careful planning and a thorough understanding of future needs.

Survival Requirement

If the grantor dies before the end of the retained interest term, the property will revert to the estate, essentially nullifying the intended tax benefits. The property would then be included in the taxable estate, potentially negating any initial savings. This makes it crucial to choose an appropriate trust term that balances tax savings with the grantor's life expectancy.

Rent

Additionally, after the trust term ends, the grantor must either vacate the property or pay fair market rent to continue living there. While paying rent to the beneficiaries can further reduce the grantor's estate, it may present practical challenges, such as strained family relationships or logistical complications in setting up rental agreements.

No Basis Step Up

When the grantor has survived the term of the QPRT, the home is no longer owned by the grantor. It is owned by the trust. When the grantor dies, therefore, the home will not be eligible for the step-up in basis at death. In the above example, when the grantor dies after 20 years, and the home is worth $2 million, assuming zero basis, if the trust sells the home after the grantor dies, the entire gain would be subject to capital gains tax.

No $250k Exclusion

If the trust holds the house until the grantor dies, it will not be eligible for the sec. 121 exclusion. This exclusion is currently $250,000 for an individual, and $500,000 for a couple, provided that the person has owned and lived in the house for two of the five years immediately preceding the sale of the house.

Generation Skipping Exemption

A QPRT is generally incompatible with effective use of the generation skipping tax exemption. The reason is that the exemption cannot be applied at the time the trust is created, but only at the time the trust concludes, and this means that the gift tax valuation discounting that the QPRT provides will not apply to generation skipping tax.

When a QPRT May Make Sense

A QPRT may make sense when the family involved does not view the limitations as serious impediments. The key limitations that will be most salient for most people include:
1. The requirement to pay rent after the QPRT term.
2. The lack of a stepped-up basis.
3. The requirement to live out the QPRT term.
4. The loss of the Section 121 exclusion.

5. Generation skipping exemption cannot be used when the trust is funded.

In most cases, these limitations will not exclude a QPRT from consideration only when all of the following conditions are met:
1. The payment of rent is seen as a positive, because it removes more money from the estate without incurring tax.
2. The long-term plan is to keep the real estate in the family, so that no sale is anticipated, and therefore the foregone basis step-up is less of an issue.
3. There is a high probability of the QPRT grantor outliving the trust term.
4. The Section 121 exclusion is not a large amount compared to the other values involved in the estate.
5. The generation skip is not important.

These conditions are most likely to be met only in relatively rare cases.

ALTERNATIVE

A QPRT will generally only be suggested in cases in which the homeowner(s) expect to have a taxable estate. In the right circumstances, typically a large, taxable estate, and a desire to keep the property in the family over the long term, a QPRT can be the right tool. But often there may be better tools for accomplishing the estate planning objectives for which a QPRT may be suggested.

Sale to An Intentionally Defective Grantor Trust

One such alternative is to sell the home to a grantor trust. Such a trust, sometimes called an intentionally defective grantor trust ("IDGT"), is for income tax purposes the same as the grantor. Thus, selling a home to such a trust does not trigger the gain recognition. The sale is usually in exchange for a note. The terms of the note, including the interest rate on the note, must meet certain rules specified by the IRS.

The sale of a house to an IDGT can serve to "freeze" the value in the estate. For example, if a house were sold for $1,000,000 note, the amount in the estate would remain

$1,000,000, but the growth in value of the house would be outside the estate. It can be beneficial to "freeze" the value if it is expected that the growth rate of the value of the real estate will be higher than the interest rate on the note.

27. Domestic Asset Protection Trusts

A Domestic Asset Protection Trust (DAPT) is an irrevocable trust established under state law (in states that permit it) that allow the trust's settlor—the person creating the trust—to also be a discretionary beneficiary while protecting the trust assets from creditors under most circumstances.

Trusts have been used for centuries to protect assets from creditors. What is new about DAPTs is that DAPTs provide asset protection for assets transferred into the trust, permitting the settlor to maintain access to those assets, often through discretionary distributions made by an independent trustee. A DAPT is typically a self-settled trust, and until fairly recently, self-settled trusts could not be protected from creditors.

Thus, the key distinguishing feature of a DAPT is that it offers protection from creditors even though the settlor retains some level of interest in the trust.

What is Special About DAPTs?

A *spendthrift* is "a person who spends improvidently or wastefully," according to Merriam Webster's dictionary. Centuries ago, trust grantors sought to put money in trust for heirs whom the grantor considered to be spendthrifts, and have the spendthrift heir disabled from spending the trust's assets profligately. Grantors (or their lawyers) accomplished this by including terms in the trust that were specifically designed to prevent the trust beneficiary from either taking too much (defined in various ways) or pledging the trust assets to a creditor.

These clauses (technically called a "disabling restraint") came to be called "spendthrift" clauses. In 1828 the first statute in the United States explicitly recognizing spendthrift clauses was enacted. "As a matter of statutory law, spendthrift trusts first arose under New York's revision of its property code in 1828."[39]

For about a hundred and fifty years, grantors frequently included a spendthrift clause when they put assets in trust.

---

[39] *Spendthrift Trusts and Public Policy: Economic and Cognitive Perspectives*, Adam J. Hirsch, Washington University Law Review, January, 1995.

But the beneficiary was always someone other than the grantor.

Asset protection trusts changed that by making it possible for a person to put assets in trust for himself (so-called "self-settled" trusts) and include a spendthrift clause.

The First Asset Protection Trusts

It is widely believed (it is hard to be certain) that trusts explicitly designed to be self-settled asset protection trusts originated in the 1980s.

In the 1980s, Denver based attorneys Barry Engel and Ron Rudman (and their law firm Engel and Rudman) persuaded the government of the Cook Islands to enact legislation recognizing self-settled asset protection trusts. I believe Engel himself helped draft the legislation, though when in the process of writing this book I called to ask him, I learned that he had died.

Soon after the Cook Islands enacted their law, other foreign jurisdictions in the British Commonwealth, or former British colonies (and hence jurisdictions that were familiar with trust law), adopted similar asset protection trust legislation. These included the Isle of Man, Nevis, and the Cayman Islands.

The idea of self-settled asset protection trusts quickly gained ground among a portion of the community of American estate planning attorneys, and it was less than ten years until an American version appeared.

Alaska – The First Domestic Asset Protection Trusts Law

The "D" in DAPT is domestic. In 1997, Alaska became the first state to adopt a trust law, the Alaska Trust Act, that enshrined self-settled asset protection trusts into law.

While it was widely reported that thousands of offshore asset protection trusts were created, and funded with an aggregate of billions of dollars, many Americans felt uncomfortable with locating their trusts in tiny jurisdictions in the middle of the ocean.

The Alaska law changed that, and there are (as of this writing) 17 US states that have some form of asset protection trust laws.

States Offering Domestic Asset Protection Trusts

In the current decade, many observers believe that the leading states for DAPTs are Nevada, Delaware, South Dakota, and Alaska. Some of the highlights of the laws of these states follow.

Nevada

Nevada is known for having some of the most favorable DAPT laws. Nevada provides a two-year statute of limitations on transfers into the trust, meaning creditors have only two years to challenge asset transfers. Additionally, Nevada does not require state income tax for assets held in the trust.

Delaware

Another popular jurisdiction for DAPTs, Delaware provides a four-year statute of limitations and is highly regarded for its strong legal framework supporting asset protection and trust administration.

South Dakota

South Dakota is known for its flexibility and favorable asset protection statutes. South Dakota has no income tax and allows perpetual trusts, making it an attractive jurisdiction for wealth preservation.

Alaska

Alaska offers a four-year statute of limitations and generally favorable trust administration laws.

KEY FEATURES OF ASSET PROTECTION TRUSTS

Asset protection trusts combine several critical features that set them apart from other asset protection structures. Among these are the following.

Irrevocable

Generally, an asset protection trust must be irrevocable. Once assets are placed in an asset protection trust, they generally cannot be removed, except under specific and often limited conditions. This irrevocable nature is essential for asset protection, as it prevents creditors from claiming assets by reversing the trust's establishment.

Discretionary Distributions

Asset protection trusts are typically structured to allow discretionary distributions to beneficiaries, including the settlor. The distributions are at the trustee's discretion, adding a layer of protection since beneficiaries have no legal right to force distributions, limiting creditor claims.

Independent Trustee Requirement

An asset protection trust must typically have an independent trustee residing in the trust's chosen jurisdiction. This requirement helps separate the settlor from control over the trust assets, and is intended to make it ineffective for a court to simply order a settler to turn over funds.

This requirement also helps explain the emergent popularity of domestic asset protection trusts, located in states like Nevada, as compared to remote island jurisdictions. As of this writing, there is at least one non-stop flight to Nevada from nearly every state in the Union.

Spendthrift Provision

It almost goes without saying that an asset protection trust includes a spendthrift clause, which restricts beneficiaries (including the settlor) from assigning their interests to creditors, ensuring the trust's assets are shielded from claims and judgment enforcement.

HOW ASSET PROTECTION TRUSTS PROTECT ASSETS

The asset protection mechanism of an asset protection trust hinges on the legal concept of separation of ownership. By transferring assets into an asset protection trust, the settlor legally gives up ownership of the assets, meaning the assets contributed are no longer legally owned by the settler. As such, those assets are not attachable even if a creditor obtains a judgment against the settler.

However, by retaining a discretionary beneficial interest, the settlor may still receive distributions under the trustee's discretion, allowing continued access to the assets without legal ownership.

This separation of ownership and beneficial interest is the cornerstone of an asset protection trust's protective capability. When structured and maintained correctly, an asset protection trust prevents most types of creditors from claiming trust assets.

Asset protection trusts are not intended to shield bad actors. As such, asset protection trusts are not entirely impervious; certain exceptions, like fraud claims and child support orders, may override DAPT protections in some cases.

LIMITATIONS AND RISKS OF ASSET PROTECTION TRUSTS

There are a number of circumstances under which an asset protection trust may fail to provide the protection sought.

Fraudulent Transfer

The concept of fraudulent transfer refers to any transfer of property without sufficient consideration made with the intent to defraud creditors. Thus, if a person has an existing claim against him, and he sets up and funds an asset protection trust, the transfer to trust is likely to be considered a fraudulent transfer. Fraudulent transfers will generally not be respected by courts.

Varying State Laws

While 17 states have some version of asset protection trust laws on their books, the remaining states do not. In states that do not have asset protection trust statutes, courts may not uphold the trust's protection provisions, especially if the settlor resides in a non- asset protection trust state.

In a case called *Waldron v. Huber*, in Washington in 2013, the court ruled against Huber. Huber had transferred property to an Alaska asset protection trust. The court refused to apply Alaska law, and instead applied Washington law, which did not recognize the validity of the self-settled trust.

Bankruptcy and Statute of Limitations

Each state has a statute of limitations on asset transfers. In the case of Alaska, that period is four years. During the period before the statute of limitations has run, transfers to a trust can be challenged. After the statute runs out, such challenges should be much more difficult.

However, federal bankruptcy law may intervene and override a state's statute period. In an Alaska case, called *Battley v. Mortensen* in 2011, the defendant, Mortensen, had established and funded an Alaska asset protection trust in 2005. Thus, Alaska's four-year statute had run by the time of the claim.

Mortensen filed for bankruptcy under chapter 7, throwing the claim (by his ex-wife) into bankruptcy court. There, a judge ruled that the federal 10-year bankruptcy statute of limitations should apply, and the trust assets were ruled reachable.

Exceptions for Certain Creditors or Public Policy

Certain claims, such as child support, alimony, or tax liabilities, may not be protected by an asset protection trust, as state laws and court orders may override the trust's provisions in these cases. In addition, there is the ever-present public policy argument that can be made.

CONCLUSION

The law and practical implementation of asset protection trusts is (in the world of trusts) relatively new. There are relatively few cases that have been decided by courts. Lawyers and others continue to develop strategies.

Anyone concerned about potential liability should, in our view, begin with insurance. The vast majority of liability claims can be covered by adequate insurance, and the insurance company should defend them.

Asset protection trusts should be considered a secondary line of defense.

For high-net-worth people, there may be better trust alternatives than an asset protection trust. Most asset protection trusts do nothing other than asset protection. They provide no insulation against income taxes, they do nothing to remove assets from a taxable estate, and they may result mainly in additional complexity that makes more effective trust planning more difficult.

28.   Offshore Asset Protection Trusts

The history of trusts designed specifically for asset protection appears to date to the mid-1980s, when the Cook Islands, a small nation in the South Pacific between Tonga and French Polynesia, adopted the International Trusts Act. The act codified a legal framework for the world's first asset protection trust specifically designed to shield assets from foreign judgments.

Though many of the movers are no longer living, it appears that the driving force behind this innovation was a group of legal professionals, including local Cook Islanders, and American Barry Engel. Engel told the author, years ago, that he played a key role in crafting the legislation, which incorporated key features like confidentiality, asset segregation, and protection against fraudulent conveyance claims.

Cayman Islands and The Bahamas

During the 1970s and 1980s, jurisdictions like the Cayman Islands and The Bahamas also began developing trust structures. While these were initially geared toward tax efficiency and estate planning, they laid the groundwork for later adaptations that incorporated asset protection provisions. The Trusts (Foreign Element) Law in the Cayman Islands, enacted in 1987, specifically addressed the enforcement of foreign judgments, marking a shift toward asset protection.

Since then, a number of jurisdictions, mostly former British colonies or British protectorates, mostly islands, have sought to improve the relative competitiveness of their financial systems by adopting legislation more favorable to offshore investors seeking to protect assets. These jurisdictions include Belize (not an island), which in 1992 adopted a Trusts Act similar to the Cook Islands' model, Nevis, the Isle of Man, and some of the Channel Islands and others.

The Belize act includes provisions for rapid trust formation and strict non-recognition of foreign judgments. Nevis, part of the Federation of Saint Kitts and Nevis, enacted the Nevis International Exempt Trust Ordinance in 1994. The Nevis ordinance, amended at least six times since adoption, is noted for features such as a short statute of limitations on fraudulent transfer claims and strict confidentiality for trust settlors and beneficiaries.

The Isle of Man, a Crown Dependency in the Irish Sea, introduced the Asset Protection Trust Act in 1995. The legislation emphasized flexibility, allowing settlors to retain significant control over trust assets while still benefiting from creditor protection.

Since the early 2000s, other jurisdictions have entered the offshore asset protection market, including Jersey, Guernsey, Singapore, and Hong Kong, each tailoring their trust laws to attract international investors. These jurisdictions have built on the original frameworks by adding advanced provisions for digital assets, hybrid trust structures, and simplified reporting requirements.

OFFSHORE VS. DOMESTIC

The trust, explicitly and primarily designed for asset protection, originated offshore because the founders of the movement had an easier time getting the desired legislation in small jurisdictions hungry to increase their share of international finance.

In an offshore asset protection trust, an individual (the grantor or settlor) transfers assets to a trust based outside his home country, and places assets under the control of a foreign trustee, subjecting them to the laws of the jurisdiction where the trust is established. The primary purpose is to create a legal barrier between the grantor's assets and potential creditors or litigants, making it significantly more challenging for these parties to access or seize the protected assets. In a properly structured trust, the assets are legally owned by the trustee, not the grantor, which forms the cornerstone of the trust's protective capabilities.

Offshore jurisdictions often do not recognize or enforce judgments from foreign courts, such as US courts, creating a hurdle for creditors attempting to access trust assets. For example, in the Cook Islands, a creditor seeking to challenge a trust must overcome a two-year statute of limitations and prove beyond a reasonable doubt that the trust was established with the intent to defraud that specific creditor.

Many offshore jurisdictions have strict confidentiality laws that prohibit the disclosure of trust details to third parties. This level of privacy can be particularly attractive to individuals concerned about potential litigation or those seeking to maintain confidentiality in their financial affairs. However, this privacy does not extend to tax reporting requirements, as U.S. citizens are still obligated to report their offshore trusts to the Internal Revenue Service (IRS) under the Foreign Account Tax Compliance Act.

EFFECTIVENESS

US law does not allow a grantor to evade existing creditors or legal obligations. Transfers to an asset protection trust must not be fraudulent, meaning they cannot be made with the intent to hinder, delay, or defraud known or potential creditors. U.S. courts have shown a willingness to pursue aggressive measures against individuals who attempt to use OAPTs to shield assets from legitimate creditors.

In *FTC v. Affordable Media, LLC*, 179 F.3d 1228 (9th Cir. 1999), the court held the defendants in contempt for failing to repatriate assets from their Cook Islands trust, rejecting their argument that compliance was impossible due to the trust's anti-duress provisions. The defendants were held to have conducted what amounted to a Ponzi scheme, and the FTC settled with the Cook Islands trustee.

The effectiveness of offshore asset protection trusts can also be impacted by domestic legal developments. The Bankruptcy Abuse Prevention and Consumer Protection Act of 2005 introduced a 10-year lookback period for asset transfers in bankruptcy cases. This extended period increases the risk that transfers to an offshore asset protection trust could be deemed fraudulent and unwound in bankruptcy proceedings.

Political and economic instability in the jurisdiction where the trust is established presents another potential risk. While many popular offshore jurisdictions have stable political environments and robust financial sectors, the possibility of sudden changes in government policy or economic conditions may be difficult for outsiders to assess.

Such instability could potentially impact the accessibility or security of trust assets.

The use of OAPTs also raises ethical considerations. Critics argue that these trusts can be used to unfairly shield assets from legitimate creditors or to evade legal responsibilities. This perception has led to increased scrutiny from regulatory bodies and a generally hostile attitude from U.S. courts towards offshore asset protection trusts. In *In re Lawrence*, 279 F.3d 1294 (11th Cir. 2002), the court affirmed a bankruptcy judge's order holding a debtor in contempt for failing to repatriate assets from an offshore trust, rejecting the impossibility defense based on the trust's structure.

U.S. REPORTING REQUIREMENTS

Americans with offshore trusts are subject to extensive reporting requirements.

U.S. tax reporting requirements for offshore trusts are complex and apply to grantors, trustees, and beneficiaries who are U.S. persons. An offshore trust may be defined as a trust established under foreign laws where a U.S. court does not have primary supervision over its administration, and U.S. persons do not control all substantial trust decisions. These requirements involve extensive disclosure to ensure compliance with tax obligations.

In general, U.S. persons who create or fund an offshore trust must file Form 3520, which reports transactions with the trust, including asset transfers, creation of the trust, or receipt of distributions. If the transfer to the offshore trust is deemed a taxable gift, Form 709, the United States Gift Tax Return, must also be filed. Additionally, under the grantor trust rules, U.S. grantors may be required to report income earned by the trust as their own, regardless of whether distributions are received.

Offshore trusts with U.S. grantors or owners must file Form 3520-A annually. This form provides the IRS with detailed information about the trust, including its income, distributions, and financial accounts. If the trustee does not file this form, the U.S. owner or grantor becomes responsible for submitting the required information to avoid penalties.

U.S. beneficiaries receiving distributions from an offshore trust must also comply with reporting requirements.

These distributions must be disclosed on Form 3520, which includes details about the amount and nature of the income received. Beneficiaries must account for any undistributed net income (UNI), which may be subject to interest charges under the throwback rules designed to prevent tax deferral through offshore trusts.

In addition to these specific forms, offshore trusts and U.S. persons associated with them may be subject to the Foreign Account Tax Compliance Act (FATCA). This legislation requires reporting of foreign financial assets exceeding certain thresholds, either directly or through the trust. Trusts holding financial accounts may also need to register with the IRS and report U.S. beneficiaries and owners.

Failure to comply with these reporting requirements can result in substantial penalties. Accurate and timely reporting can avoid complications, and professional advice is often recommended to navigate the intricate reporting obligations for offshore trusts.

WHEN TO USE

Because of the extensive availability of domestic asset protection trust laws, especially in states including Nevada, South Dakota, and Alaska, the use of a foreign asset protection trust may be seen as a red flag by some judges.

If a potential grantor does not have current creditors, and the transfer of assets to an asset protection trust will not be fraudulent, the choice between domestic and offshore is a judgment call that should be made in consultation with informed professionals, and taking into account as much information about the situation, the potential threats, and the benefits and costs involved in each potential alternative.

29. Purpose Trusts

The term "purpose trust" or "special purpose trust" refers to a type of trust that, rather than having specified beneficiaries, is intended to provide for a particular purpose. Perhaps the most common type of purpose trust in use today is a pet trust.

Why is it Called a "Purpose" Trust?

Trusts derive from the common law tradition, going all the way back to medieval England. Under the common law, a trust is not a business or a company in the way that a corporation or an LLC is. Rather, a trust is a settlement of property, by a grantor, to a trustee. But while the trustee legally owns the property, the trustee is not (usually) the so-called beneficiary, or beneficial owner. The beneficial owner is the person or people who are entitled to enjoy the fruits of the property.

Under the common law, a trust must have at least one identifiable beneficiary. The trustee(s) then manage the trust's property for the benefit of the beneficiary, rather, for example, than for the trustee's own benefit. Under this arrangement, a trustee has a fiduciary obligation to the beneficiary. And because the beneficiary is a person, the beneficiary can (at least in theory) seek to enforce the terms of the trust if the trustee were perceived to not be doing a proper job.

But a purpose trust has no identifiable beneficiary. Thus, it would seem, a purpose trust cannot exist under the common law. While charitable trusts might be considered to be a special type of purpose trust, they have their own law and we do not deal with charitable trusts in this chapter.

Purpose trusts are possible because they are recognized by legislated laws, or statutes.[40]

---

[40] Though for the present purposes we don't care much whether the laws result from the common law or from legislation, from a larger social perspective the difference can be very significant. The great 20th century polymath and Nobel Prize recipient in economics, Friedrich Hayek, wrote a three-volume trilogy titled *Law, Legislation and Liberty* on the general topic. Volume 2, *The Mirage of Social Justice*, should be required reading for everyone who has anything to do with legislation. Hayek's analysis explains why the mad pursuit of "social

Statute is Broad

Because (with certain exceptions) a purpose trust could not exist under the common law, and because enough people had enough reasons to seek legislation, most states now have legislation that explicitly recognizes purpose trusts.

While the statutes differ from state to state, most are modeled on the Uniform Trust Code (UTC), which states, in part, that "that the trust have a purpose that is lawful, not contrary to public policy, and possible to achieve."[41]

This language leaves the possibility of creating trusts for a wide variety of purposes. The UTC has a section, 408, dealing with trusts "for the care of an animal" which are commonly known as "pet trusts" and another more catchall section, 409, dealing with "noncharitable trust[s] without ascertainable beneficiaries."

MAJOR CATEGORIES OF PURPOSE TRUSTS

In an article in Tax-Notes, a list of common purposes of purpose trusts appears. The following is a subset of that list.

1. Stewardship
2. Employee ownership
3. Maintenance of a collection
4. Promotion of a non-charitable cause
5. Maintenance of gravesites
6. Cryogenic trusts
7. To own off-balance-sheet assets[42]

"Stewardship"

The idea of applying so-called "stewardship" is gaining some traction, particularly among some left-leaning billionaires, as a way to impose their political stamp on their companies, even after they are gone. In essence, the idea is to separate the voting control of the business from the bulk of the economic value, and vest that voting control in the hands of "stewards" who are (by magical thinking?)

---

justice" is wrongheaded from its very inception, and can only result in the loss of liberty, as indeed it has already.

[41] Uniform Trust Code, Sec. 105(b)(3)

[42] *Purpose Trusts and Steward Ownership*, Ellen K. Harrison, Tax Notes, May, 2024

somehow expected to protect the interests of everyone touched in any way by the business, even at the expense of shareholder returns.

The idea that a business should be run for the benefit of anyone other than the shareholders is, in our view, dangerous, inefficient, and almost certainly a violation of the controlling shareholders' and managers' fiduciary duties. Nevertheless, it appears that this is happening with certain companies, such as Patagonia. Caveat shareholder.

Stewardship = Breach of Fiduciary?

We believe that there is a strong prima-facie case that the "stewardship" concept is almost synonymous with breach of fiduciary of obligation. This may be particularly true when "stewardship" is applied by left-leaning corporate directors or via a stewardship trust. The reason is that by definition a fiduciary obligation applies to people who are managing a company. They owe, by definition, the fiduciary duty to the owners—the shareholders. This is how the US Consumer Financial Protection Bureau—the brainchild of US senator Elizabeth Warren, defines the obligation:

"A fiduciary is someone who manages money or property for someone else. When you're named a fiduciary and accept the role, you must—by law—manage the person's money and property for their benefit, not yours.[43]"

And, lest there be any doubt, a fiduciary must,

"Act only in their [the owners'] best interest. Because you are dealing with someone else's money and property, your duty is to make decisions that are best for them, not you."

Employee Ownership Trust

Many readers will be familiar with the idea of an ESOP or Employee Stock Ownership Plan as a way to own a business. ESOPs are ERISA retirement plans, and are different from the "Employee Ownership Trust" or EOT.

---

[43] https://www.consumerfinance.gov/ask-cfpb/what-is-a-fiduciary-en-1769/#:~:text=A%20fiduciary%20is%20someone%20who,their%20money%20and%20property%20separate.

ESOPs, being ERISA plans, have very complex rules, subject the company to heavy oversight from the Department of Justice, and offer a complex set of tax rules which may, or may not, end up benefiting employees.

Employee Ownership Trusts are intended to provide some of the benefits without some of the costs and burdens of an ESOP plan.

Maintenance of a Collection

Many people, over the course of a lifetime, acquire significant collections of valuable items such as books, guns, artwork, antiques, cars, or other specialized items, and they would like to see the collections kept intact and maintained after their deaths. If the collection is appropriate, valuable enough, it may be possible to contribute the collection to a museum, or even create a museum.

Even though you may have spent a good chunk of your life, and money, building a collection, the hard fact is that most museums will not agree to keep most collections intact. And it can be very expensive to create and maintain a museum.

So, a purpose trust, provided sufficient funds are available, can do the job.

Promotion of Non-Charitable Cause

There are a number of causes that people are passionate about which do not themselves qualify as "charitable" under the Internal Revenue Code. Thus, a non-charitable cause cannot be supported by a charitable trust.

But such causes can be supported by a non-charitable, purpose trust. Examples of such causes are as varied as there are people with causes, but some of the more common ones might be promoting certain activities or games, genres of writing such as journalism, or community activities, celebrations or festivals.

Gravesites

While many cemeteries are owned and operated by tax-exempt institutions, such as a church or synagogue, the special maintenance of individual gravesites is not a tax-exempt activity.

Cryogenics

In his 1956 novel *The Door into Summer*, science fiction author Robert A Heinlein makes extensive plot use of the concept of "cold sleep." The idea is that by reducing a person's body temperature low enough, it would be possible to preserve that person, intact, long into the future, and revive him in that distant future.

The idea gained some popular currency in the 1960s and in 1967, James Bedford, a professor at UC Berkeley (where else?) died and became the first person to be cryogenically frozen.

As of this writing, no one has been revived. (I bet you already knew that!)

The idea primarily appeals to certain rich people, and they have thought about how to preserve assets.

Off-Balance-Sheet Assets

This use of a purpose trust appears to us like it might be another instance of trying to separate the control of a public company from those public shareholders, and vest control (or control over certain aspects) in a non-public entity. Meta (formerly Facebook) reportedly has an "Oversight Board Trust" whose purpose is "to facilitate the creation, funding, management and oversight of a structure that will permit and protect the operation of an Oversight Board for Content Decisions . . . whose purpose is to protect free expression by making principled, independent decisions about important pieces of content and by issuing policy advisory opinions on . . . content policies."[44]

OTHER CONSIDERATIONS

Trust Term

Until the early 1980s, non-charitable trusts could not last "forever" because of the "rule against perpetuities." The rule against perpetuities is a common law concept from the law of property stating that an interest in land or real property must vest no later than 21 years after the death of a life-in-being (i.e. a real person who is alive when the trust is created) or the claim to the real property is not valid.

---

[44] https://about.fb.com/wp-content/uploads/2019/09/oversight_board_charter.pdf

The "Royalty Lives Clause"

The rule against perpetuities gave rise to the phenomenon, particularly in Britain, of trusts that included clauses such as the following

"…ending on the expiration of 21 years after the death of the last survivor of the lineal descendants of Queen Victoria living at the time of my death".[45]

In 1983, South Dakota enacted a statute that permits a trust to have perpetual life. Other states followed suit. Florida, for example, caps the trust life at 1000 years.

Trust Protector

The attentive reader will have noticed that we frequently talk of a trust's grantor, beneficiaries, and trustee, and indeed every trust (except purpose trusts) have all three of these.

In recent years, particularly following the Uniform Trust Code section 808 (b)-(d), another role called "Trust Protector" has been appearing in more and more trusts. The role of the trust protector is, more or less, to "watch the watcher." That is, the trust protector is tasked with ensuring that the trustee does what he is supposed to do to be an additional voice ensuring that the trust accomplishes the purpose set out by the grantor.

There is little case law on the powers and limitations of trust protectors, as protectors really only started appearing in meaningful numbers in the 1990s.[46]

A trust protector may help ensure the trust achieves the grantor's goals, even if the law changes and an "irrevocable" trust needs to be amended to achieve those goals.

COURT EXPOSURE

Any trust that lasts long enough has the potential to be exposed to the ruling of a court that believes the court's judgment (in the non-legal sense of the word) should supersede that of the trustee or the grantor. As such, there is

---

[45] https://www.birketts.co.uk/legal-update/royal-lives-clause-is-your-trust-running-out-of-time/#:~:text=An%20example%20would%20be%20a,yet%20have%20started%20to%20run.

[46] *Trust Protectors, Why They Have Become "The Next Big Thing"*, Lawrence A. Frolick, University of Pittsburgh School of Law.

the risk, that probably grows with time, of a court or judge overturning part or all of the purpose of the trust, if the court or judge doesn't approve.

One such way that could happen is that the court could rule that the trust has "excessive" funds to carry out the trust's purpose, and the court might order that some of the trust's assets be diverted to a different purpose, or to a party with standing.

In Tennessee, for example, a grantor's descendants would likely have standing if they could show that the trust had been funded excessively. Thus, a grantor seeking to ensure that his or her desires are followed may want to carefully select the jurisdiction for a purpose trust, and have it drafted with sufficient attention paid to the potential for a court to divert trust assets to other purposes.

30.   Pet Trusts

A Pet Trust is a particular kind of purpose trust. Pet trusts are specifically discussed and described in section 408 of the Uniform Trust Act. As of this writing, all 50 states recognize the validity of pet trusts.

A pet trust, like other trusts, must have a grantor, a trustee, and should have a description of how you would like the trust to work. A trust could provide for the care of a specific animal, or it could provide for a class of animals.

Specific Animal

If you desire to provide only for a specific animal, you would aim to describe that animal unambiguously in the trust. This might be done by reference to the animal by name, provided that at least one responsible person will know what animal is meant, or by other means such as pictures, or by having the animal microchipped and referring to the microchip data, or even by DNA sampling.

All Pets

More commonly, people will create a pet trust to provide for the ongoing care of all their pets after the grantor is gone. This can be done by referring to the pets as a class.

STANDARD OF CARE

Not everyone treats their pets the same as everyone else does. Some people, for example, allow their pets in their homes, in their beds, and treat the pet very much like they would treat a child. Others treat their pets differently.

While most or all jurisdictions have laws for the minimum standards of care for pets, most people who care enough to create a pet trust will probably want to specify the level or standard which they would like to ensure for their pets. Among the considerations, and suggested standards, when drafting (or having the trust drafted) are the following.

The level and specificity of the instructions may depend on who is going to care for the animal, and in what conditions. Someone who takes over care of a pet dog, and cares for the dog in their own home, may require different instructions than would be appropriate if the dog were to be housed in a commercial facility.

Housing: It should be safe, secure, clean, sanitary and in good repair.

Space: Animals sleeping quarters should have enough space to move around, sit, stand, and lie down. Animals should also have, or have access to, sufficient space to perform the activities natural and customary for such animals. Horses, for example, should have access to plenty of space to run and frolic, appropriate to the type of life most congenial to that type of animal.

Activity: Animals should continue to have the opportunity to the levels of activity to which they are accustomed, or in the case of elderly people who have not been able to provide their pets with sufficient activity, to the level of activity which is natural to the type of animal.

Food and water: Animals should have access to fresh, species appropriate food and water. It is questionable whether, in the case of certain domesticated animals, that diet should include certain commercially available "pet foods" that may reflect certain human biases at the expense of the animal's well-being. An example might be "vegan cat food." Cats are obligate carnivores, meaning they must eat meat, and therefore putting them on a vegan diet is likely cruel.[47]

Bedding: Bedding should be appropriate for the animal and free of substances that could injure them.

Temperature and humidity: The environment should be appropriate for the species of animal.

Ventilation: Facilities should have adequate ventilation.

Lighting: Lighting should be appropriate for the species and allow for good observation of the animals.

Veterinary care: Depending on the type of animal and the lifestyle to which the animal is accustomed, grantors may wish to provide instructions that their animals should receive medically indicated veterinary care, which could include vaccinations and parasite control.

Records: Facilities should keep records of all veterinary care for each animal.

---

[47] https://vetmed.tamu.edu/news/pet-talk/cats-are-carnivores-so-they-should-eat-like-one/

Funding

The standard (and not very useful) recommendation is to provide "adequate" funding. To the extent that a grantor's resources permit, it would be preferable (from the animals' point of view) to overfund the trust, and when the last animal dies direct the remaining funds to other beneficiaries, than to underfund the trust.

Final Instructions

Some people may wish to provide instructions specifying what should be done when the animal dies, and may also wish to provide guidance regarding whether to shorten the animal's suffering in the event that the animal becomes unable to live pain-free.

STATE OVERVIEW

The following is a list showing the key features of pet trust laws by state.[48]

Alabama

Trust for animals alive during settlor's lifetime; terminates upon death of last animal.

Alaska

Trust for designated domestic/pet animals; terminates when no living animal covered or after 21 years.

Arizona

Trust for animals alive during settlor's lifetime; terminates upon death of last animal.

Arkansas

Trust for animals alive during settlor's lifetime; terminates upon death of last animal.

California

Trust for animals alive during settlor's lifetime; terminates upon death of last animal unless specified otherwise.

---

[48] This list is based on data compiled by the American Society for the Prevention of Cruelty to Animals, and has not been independently verified.

Colorado

Trust for designated domestic/pet animals and offspring in gestation; terminates when no living animal covered.

Connecticut

Trust for animals alive during settlor's lifetime; terminates upon death of last animal; requires "trust protector".

Delaware

Trust for specific animals alive during trustor's lifetime; terminates when no living animal covered.

District of Columbia

Trust for animals alive during settlor's lifetime; terminates upon death of last animal.

Florida

Trust for animals alive during settlor's lifetime; terminates upon death of last animal.

Georgia

Trust for animals alive during settlor's lifetime; terminates upon death of last animal.

Hawaii

Trust for designated domestic/pet animals; terminates when no living animal covered.

Idaho

Purpose trust for animal care; no specific termination clause mentioned.

Illinois

Trust for designated domestic/pet animals; terminates when no living animal covered.

Indiana

Trust for animals alive during settlor's lifetime; terminates upon death of last animal.

Iowa

Trust for animals alive during settlor's lifetime; terminates when no living animal covered.

Kansas

Trust for animals alive during settlor's lifetime; terminates upon death of last animal.

Kentucky

Trust for animals alive during settlor's lifetime; terminates upon death of last animal.

Louisiana

Trust for animals alive during settlor's lifetime; terminates upon death of last animal.

Maine

Trust for animals alive during settlor's lifetime; terminates upon death of last animal.

Maryland

Trust for animals alive during settlor's lifetime; terminates upon death of last animal.

Massachusetts

Trust for animals alive during settlor's lifetime; terminates upon death of last animal unless specified otherwise.

Michigan

Trust for designated domestic/pet animals; terminates when no living animal covered or after 21 years.

Minnesota

Trust for animals alive during settlor's lifetime; terminates upon death of animals or after 90 years.

Mississippi

Trust for animals alive during settlor's lifetime; terminates upon death of last animal.

Missouri

Trust for animals alive during settlor's lifetime; terminates upon death of last animal.

Montana

Trust for designated domestic/pet animals; terminates when no living animal covered or after 21 years.

Nebraska

Trust for animals alive during settlor's lifetime; terminates upon death of last animal.

Nevada

Trust for animals alive during settlor's lifetime; terminates when no living animal covered.

New Hampshire

Trust for animals alive during settlor's lifetime; terminates upon death of last animal.

New Jersey

Trust for domesticated animals; terminates when no living animal covered.

New Mexico

Trust for animals alive during settlor's lifetime; terminates upon death of last animal.

New York

Trust for designated domestic/pet animals; terminates when no living animal beneficiary.

North Carolina

Trust for designated domestic/pet animals alive at trust creation; terminates upon death of last animal.

North Dakota

Trust for animals alive during settlor's lifetime; terminates upon death of last animal.

Ohio

Trust for animals alive during settlor's lifetime; terminates upon death of last animal.

Oklahoma

Trust for designated domestic/pet animals; terminates when no living animal covered unless specified otherwise.

Oregon

Trust for animals alive during settlor's lifetime; terminates upon death of last animal.

Pennsylvania

Trust for animals alive during settlor's lifetime; terminates upon death of last animal.

Rhode Island

Trust for animals alive during settlor's lifetime; terminates upon death of last animal.

South Carolina

Trust for animals alive or in gestation during settlor's lifetime; terminates upon death of last animal.

South Dakota

Trust for designated animals; terminates when no living animal covered.

Tennessee

Trust for animals alive during settlor's lifetime; terminates upon death of last animal or after 90 years.

Texas

Trust for animals alive during settlor's lifetime; terminates upon death of last animal.

Utah

Trust for designated domestic/pet animals; terminates when no living animal covered.

Vermont

Trust for animals alive during grantor's lifetime; terminates upon death of last animal.

Virginia

Trust for animals alive during settlor's lifetime; terminates upon death of last animal; allows for post-death expenses.

Washington

Trust for one or more animals; terminates when no living animal covered or after 150 years unless specified otherwise.

West Virginia

Trust for animals alive during settlor's lifetime; terminates upon death of last animal.

Wisconsin

Trust for animals alive during settlor's lifetime; terminates upon death of last animal.

Wyoming

Trust for animals alive during settlor's lifetime; terminates upon death of last animal.

31. Gun Trusts

A "Gun Trust" or "NFA Trust" is a trust created for the specific purpose of owning (and perhaps purchasing) certain property that is regulated under the National Firearms Act. This law specifically identifies machine guns, so-called 'short-barreled rifles', suppressors and certain other 'destructive devices' as requiring an extra level of scrutiny and paperwork, as compared to rifles, shotguns and handguns.

National Firearms Act ("NFA"), which is 26 U.S.C. § 5845(f), for example, defines a destructive device as:

"(1) any explosive, incendiary, or poison gas, (A) bomb, (B) grenade, (C) rocket having a propellant charge of more than 4 ounces, (D) missile having an explosive charge of more than 1/4 ounce, (E) mine or (F) similar device."

If you don't own any of these items (machine guns, short-barreled rifles, suppressors or 'destructive devices') you probably don't need, and wouldn't benefit from, a gun trust.

Terminology

For the purposes of this discussion, (and following the usage of the National Firearms Act) the term NFA firearm will include those items identified by the NFA. These are, approximately,

"fully-automatic firearms (termed "machineguns"), rifles and shotguns that have an overall length under 26 inches, rifles with a barrel under 16 inches, shotguns with a barrel under 18 inches, and firearm sound suppressors (termed "silencers"). The Gun Control Act of 1968 (GCA) placed "destructive devices" (primarily explosives and the like, but also including firearms over .50 caliber, other than most shotguns)."[49]

Notice that this list includes things that in normal speech most people would not consider to be "firearms". Among these are suppressors (often called "silencers"), and the above catalogued destructive devices.

Incidentally, and having absolutely nothing to do with "trust" in the legal sense, the Hollywood depiction of the effectiveness of suppressors is wildly inaccurate. Hollywood typically depicts a silenced pistol as making about as much noise as a quiet whisper.

---

[49] https://www.nraila.org/get-the-facts/national-firearms-act-nfa/

A whisper is typically about 20 to 30 decibels. In the movies, the "silenced" pistols are typically 9mm semi-automatics. Unsilenced, the muzzle blast of a 9mm pistol will be in the neighborhood of 160 decibels.[50] Even silenced, however, that same 9mm muzzle blast would register about 125 decibels.[51] And for reference, 125 decibels is a level of noise greater than a pneumatic wood chipper, but less than a jet engine![52]

WHY USE A GUN TRUST?

Approximately 42% of American households report owning at least one gun.[53] Nevertheless, most gun owners have probably never even heard of a gun trust. So why do people use gun trusts?

The short answer is that the use of a gun trust can make it easier to comply with the Byzantine terms of the National Firearms Act, and make it less likely that the owner of the regulated item will accidentally fail to comply.

Don't Touch!

The National Firearms Act, among other things, regulates the "transfer" of covered items. You might not think that lending a silencer to a friend would constitute a "transfer" but the BATF (the federal Bureau of Alcohol, Tobacco and Firearms) does. Here, in part, is how they define "transfer":

Section 9.1 Definition of "transfer." The term "transfer" is broadly defined by the NFA to include "selling, assigning, pledging, leasing, loaning, giving away, or otherwise disposing of" an NFA firearm.165 The lawful transfer of an NFA firearm generally requires the filing of an appropriate transfer form with ATF, payment of any transfer tax imposed, approval of the form by ATF, and registration of the firearm to the transferee in the NFRTR. Approval must be obtained before a transfer may be made.

However, that does not mean that you can never let your friend handle your NFA item. The BATF, in a non-binding letter to an inquirer, has stated:

---

[50] https://proears.com/loudest-guns/#:~:text=The%20lowly%209mm%20Luger%20fired,to%20cause%20immediate%20hearing%20damage.

[51] https://www.thearmorylife.com/silence-is-golden-gsl-9mm-stealth-suppressor-review/

[52] https://ehs.yale.edu/sites/default/files/files/decibel-level-chart.pdf

[53] https://www.pewresearch.org/short-reads/2024/07/24/key-facts-about-americans-and-guns/#:~:text=Measuring%20gun%20ownership,reported%20they%20owned%20a%20gun.

"A transfer does not occur if in the presence of the owner of the weapon, another party uses or examines the weapon. The weapon must never leave the sight of the owner and must be returned to the owner as soon as any examination or usage is completed."[54]

The purpose of a gun trust is to make it less of a hassle to purchase, own, and transfer NFA firearms requiring an ATF-4 form.

WHAT IS A GUN TRUST?

There is no legal definition of a "gun trust." Rather, a gun trust is a trust that is designed primarily for the purpose of acquiring and owning "NFA" firearms. In most cases, a gun trust will be a revocable trust. The grantor will be the person who wants to "own" the NFA firearm, and the trustee will be the grantor and perhaps a spouse.

Primary Benefits of a Gun Trust

Gun trusts offer several benefits. The most important of these include:
1. Facilitation of purchase
2. Facilitation of multiple user access
3. Facilitation of transfer on death

Purchase

For the first NFA firearm purchased, even using a gun trust, the purchaser will have to go through the whole panoply of regulatory filings. But using a gun trust may facilitate the purchase of subsequent items, by reducing the amount of paperwork required for each purchase, as compared to purchasing the items as an individual.

Multiple User Access

NFA firearms may have only a single owner, but that owner can be a trust. The trustees of a gun trust can have access to the item. Thus, for example, a husband may buy a silencer and make the gun trust the actual purchaser and owner. The husband and wife can be trustees. Both would have to go through the full paperwork, including background check and fingerprinting. Both can then legally use the item without the other present.

---

[54] Letter dated Jan. 10, 2014, signed by Edward D. Saavedra, Jr., and reproduced on thetruthaboutguns.com website. Retrieved 12/1/2024.

Transfer on Death

When an individual dies, his or her property passes by will (which may or may not involve probate) to the person's heirs. In the case of NFA firearms, people may wish to avoid the hassle of filing an ATF Form 5 to transfer the ownership from the decedent to the heir. A trust avoids this additional paperwork.

KEY ELEMENTS

A gun trust has the same basic elements as other trusts. It has a grantor, a trustee, property, beneficiaries, and a number of provisions determining rights and restrictions concerning the operations of the trust.

Customization and State Compliance

Despite the fact that firearm ownership is a right specified in the US Constitution, many states have a plethora of laws regarding firearms. Those laws vary from state to state. Thus, it likely behooves a grantor to consider state law to help ensure that a gun trust complies with laws of the relevant state(s) involved.

Comparison to LLCs or Corporations

In theory it would be possible to use an LLC or corporation in place of a gun trust. There are several reasons most people prefer to use a trust. These include:
1. Costs
2. Privacy
3. Flexibility
4. Transfer on Death

Costs

A trust can be created without a required payment to the state, whereas every state requires an up-front fee to grant an LLC or corporate charter. In addition, most states impose ongoing annual fees to maintain an LLC or corporation. Some states also impose annual minimum taxes on corporations or LLCs, even if there is no income.

Privacy

The federal corporate transparency act requires that LLCs and corporations report certain information regarding so-called beneficial ownership. These requirements do not apply to trusts.

Flexibility

A trust does not have to be registered with a state, whereas an LLC or corporation does. If you move to another state, an LLC or corporation may have to reregister, unlike a trust.

Transfer on Death

Trusts, by their nature, are designed to facilitate the transfer of assets on the death of the grantor. LLCs and corporations offer no such built-in help.

NFA gun trusts provide a versatile framework for owning, using, and transferring NFA firearms. They can offer advantages in terms of shared possession, estate planning, and asset protection. As with most legal documents, it is advisable to work with knowledgeable professionals to ensure proper setup and ongoing compliance with applicable laws and regulations.

32. Cryonic Preservation Trusts

A cryogenic, or cryonic, preservation trust is a Purpose Trust for the specialized purpose of providing for the frozen (cryogenic) preservation of a dead person's body (or in some cases only the head).

In 1826, the British reading public was transfixed by the story of Roger Dodsworth. Dodsworth was born in 1585, and became a well-known antiquary. (An antiquary is someone who studies and/or collects antiquities.)

The story, reported first by newspapers on the continent, and then picked up by London newspapers, told of the fate of Dodsworth. The papers reported that Dodsworth had been on an expedition to the Saint Gothard region of the Swiss Alps in the 1660s, when he had been buried by an avalanche, and presumed dead. What was deemed newsworthy in 1826 (as indeed it would be today), was that Dodsworth's body had been discovered, and thawed, and Dodsworth brought back to life.

Of course, the Dodsworth story proved to be a hoax.

But the dream of freezing and eventually reviving the dead lives on.

CRYONIC SUSPENSION

The modern guise is generally known by the term *cryonic suspension*. The law forbids freezing a body until its owner is deemed legally dead. Thus, technically the person cannot be "cryonically suspended" or placed in "suspended animation" as occurs in many modern science fiction stories.

Everyone involved acknowledges that only dead people are frozen. (In the entire world, there are an estimated 300 or so people who have died and had all or part of their bodies frozen in cryonic suspension.)

Eccentric Millionaires, Bizarre Stories

Cryonic suspension is relatively expensive, and completely unproven. While detailed demographic data are not publicly available, reports indicate that the process can cost in the range of $30,000 to $200,000 or more.

Electing to have yourself frozen has proven in some cases to be controversial. Anyone planning to have it done should probably check with heirs, and obtain their buy-in well in advance of need. One reason for such "pre-need" planning is to prevent post-death squabbling and potential litigation, which in addition to being unpleasant and expensive, can interfere with the freezing process.

The most famous person to have his body frozen is former baseball star Ted Williams. Williams died in 2002 in Florida at age 83. Because of Williams' celebrity status, the story of his death, his cryonic suspension, and surrounding claims and controversies, became national news.

CBS reported[55] that after Williams died, his body was flown (by private jet) to Arizona, for cryonic suspension. He was decapitated, his head frozen in one container, and his body in another. One of his daughters sued to try to prevent the procedure, claiming that his wish had been to be cremated and his ashes distributed in Florida. She settled for cash instead.

Years later, in 2009, a former employee of the cryonics facility published a book called *Frozen: My Journey into the World of Cryonics, Deception and Death*. ESPN reported that the book's author claimed, among other things, to have seen an employee "swing a monkey wrench at Williams' frozen severed head to try to remove a tuna can stuck to it."[56] (Apparently the practice was to use tuna cans as "pedestals" to support the frozen head. It wasn't clear whether the can still contained tuna.)

FREEZING ISN'T REALLY THE ISSUE, REVIVIFICATION IS

A couple moments of reflection reveals that getting frozen isn't the real goal. The real goal is to get brought back to life.

Even setting aside the technical details (as of this writing, there is not even a plausible hypothesis about how this age-old dream could be realized), there are significant economic and legal issues to consider. However, we can consider some of the potential issues that may arise during the period of cryonic suspension.

ECONOMICS

The economics of cryonic suspension can be considered in three phases. These are:
1. Suspension phase
2. Revivification phase
3. Second life phase

---

[55] https://www.cbsnews.com/news/ted-williams-frozen-in-two-pieces/
[56] https://www.espn.com/boston/mlb/news/story?id=4524957

Suspension

The first phase is the easiest to analyze, because it actually occurs now. The analysis of this first phase is similar to the way we think about (from an economic point of view) a burial.

In a standard burial, there is the preparation of the corpse and the grave, interment, and then maintenance (or not) of the burial site.

In the case of cryonic suspension, the dead body is prepared, prior to freezing. Current practice is to remove as much of the blood as possible, and replace it with what amounts to anti-freeze, and cool the body as quickly as possible without causing tissues to develop ice crystals.

Instead of burial, the prepared body is placed into a large container (analogous to a giant thermos) and cooled, inside the insulated storage container, to the temperature of liquid nitrogen, about negative 196 degrees Celsius.

The selection of -196 degrees is an economic decision, not a scientific one. Under current technology, it is feasible to cool and store medical items using liquid nitrogen. At recent market prices, liquid nitrogen averages about $1 per liter. Liquid nitrogen can be produced from regular air (which is 79% nitrogen) using commercially available machinery. According to one vendor, using their equipment brings the cost down to $0.18 per liter.[57]

Liquid helium, by contrast, is much more expensive, (recently $40 per liter), more difficult to work with, and much colder. Thus, the choice of liquid nitrogen, and its temperature of negative 196 degrees Celsius, is not based on any science or evidence of effectiveness, but rather on cost.

Current Practice

As of this writing, there are several vendors offering cryonic suspension. The common practice seems to be that you become a "member" of the organization during life, for which you pay a modest annual fee. There is then a one-time lump sum to pay for the procedure and then to keep the body frozen "forever."

This practice is similar in concept to the purchase of a burial plot which includes maintenance "forever."

Revivification

Because no one has a clue about how (or if) it will be possible to revive a frozen corpse, for the time being the price of doing so is infinite. Will that price ever come down? No one knows.

---

[57] https://www.rutherfordtitan.com/liquid-nitrogen-generators/liquid-nitrogen-price-usa/

Second Life

In discussions that I have had over the years with people who considered having their bodies frozen post death, the main concern was how, and whether, they could preserve some of their wealth for their use after they were revived.

The remainder of this chapter deals with how such wealth might be preserved.

PRESERVING WEALTH FOR SECOND LIFE

Under current US legal structures, a purpose trust for the purpose of maintaining a body in cryonic suspension is possible. The purpose can be stated, and a trustee can carry out the task.

But what about reviving the corpse, and then providing wealth for the revived dead person?

Revival

The actual revival of a frozen corpse could be a valid purpose of a purpose trust. For obvious reasons, there is no actual law on this point.

Let's assume that revival becomes technically feasible. What incentives could/should a trust offer for the revival of a dead person?

There are at least several issues that come to mind. These include the risk of revival, the cost of revival, and creating an incentive to revive the person at all.

Risk

If and when technology to revive from cryogenic storage is created, it will likely develop over time. Furthermore, it may develop slowly. It may be far from obvious how fast it will develop, or how good it will ever get.

Suppose that you are writing the terms for how you want your trustee to revive you. Suppose technology develops that "could" work. Would you want your trustee to have you revived? What if there's a 10% chance of success? 20%? All the way up to close to 100%? At what point should your trustee "pull the trigger"?

There are no obviously right or wrong answers.

Timing

You might go through a similar analysis with regard to timing. Assuming revival becomes technically feasible, would you want to be revived as soon as possible? As soon as it's "certain" that you can be revived? Would you want your trustee to consider then-prevailing social conditions?

What if there are then prejudices against revived people? What if they don't have rights or full rights, or citizenship?

Again, it seems to us, there are no obviously right or wrong answers.

Getting Your Wealth Back

Under current and historic law, there is no provision for restoring property to someone after he's been dead for a long time. But such a law could occur in the future, and we see no reason why you couldn't put language into a trust directing your trustee to restore your wealth to you, or make you a trust beneficiary, when and if you are revived.

Trust Term

The trust term for a revivification trust should be perpetual. There is simply no way of knowing when, if ever, revival will be possible. It could take a hundred years, five hundred, a thousand, or it may never happen. So, a perpetual trust seems the way to go.

Tax

Taxes constitute one of the greatest barriers to long term wealth preservation. Among these, the income tax and the estate/gift tax are dominant. A non-charitable trust, such as a revival trust, will be subject to income taxes. Perhaps the best that can be done along those lines is to instruct the trustee or investment manager to invest the trust assets for the long term with the goal of maximizing long-term after-tax wealth.

With respect to the gift and estate tax, it may be possible to fund the trust with assets that qualify for the generation skipping tax exemption, and apply that exemption.

WHAT IS THE LEGAL IDENTITY OF THE REVIVED PERSON?

If revivals ever become reality, society will at that time have to deal with the issue of the identity of the revived person. Is it the same person? Or is it a different person? Do we end up creating new categories that have not been even considered before?

This question touches on, but is not quite the same as, the age-old philosophical question of personal identity. There is a long and inconclusive literature on this subject, going back at least to John Locke's An Essay Concerning Human Understanding (1694).

While it has been an issue of philosophical concern, the law has always been pretty clear in identifying a particular person with a specific body.

Choice of Law and Jurisdiction

Because we cannot know how (or if) the law of identity or of revival will develop, it may make sense to give your trustee the broadest possible powers to select the law and the jurisdiction in the future.

Adverse Parties

A difficult issue to deal with may be how to provide for (or protect against) potential claimants who may have an adverse interest to that of the potentially revived person. Most purpose trusts, or the law governing them, provides for who can benefit from trust property if the purpose of the trust cannot be fulfilled.

Imagine, if you can, that your body is frozen, successfully, for a thousand years. Imagine further than 1000 years from now, your trust is still intact. Your initial funding of $1 million has compounded at 1% per year, after taxes and expenses. That trust principal has grown to $21 billion.

Suppose further that there are a thousand people who trace their ancestry back to you, and therefore have a claim to be your legal heirs.

You might not want those people to have a say in whether you can or should be revived, because they might have an economic incentive to see to it that you are not revived.

STRANGER IN A STRANGE LAND

In 1670, the French philosopher and mathematician Blaise Pascal proposed what he saw as an irrefutable argument in favor of the belief in God. He argued that you had a binary choice, either believe in God, or disbelieve. He further argued that if you believe in God and are correct, the reward is eternal bliss. And if you do not believe in God, and you are right, you gain nothing. Against that, he argued that if you believe in God and are wrong, you lose nothing, while if you disbelieve in God and are wrong, you spend eternity in hell.

He presented this as a "no brainer" argument that would persuade any rational person to choose belief in God.

Similarly, some people today make a similar argument regarding cryonics. Without it, they say, you're certainly dead forever. (The people who make this argument would typically not believe in any form of afterlife, such as heaven.) But, the argument goes, you might as well try cryonics because you have nothing to lose.

Over the years, many people have poked many holes in Pascal's argument. But the central idea of a proposition with big potential upside and no downside (as he presents the proposition "believe in God"), may appeal to some people as an argument for cryonic suspension, and for the use of a cryonic suspension and revivification trust.

However, one huge difference is that while Pascal promised Heaven, cryonics promises, at best, that if it all works, you'll be a "stranger in a strange land."[58]

---

[58] If you recognize this phrase, depending on your experience, you may associate it either with the King James translation of Exodus 2:22, or with the Robert Heinlein science fiction novel of the same name. The original Hebrew translates more accurately as "stranger in an alien land" which is even more appropriate for our use here. (גֵּר הָיִיתִי בְּאֶרֶץ נָכְרִיָּה)

33. Understanding ILITs

An Irrevocable Life Insurance Trust (ILIT) is a type of trust specifically designed to own and manage a life insurance policy independently of the insured person's estate. The "irrevocable" nature of an ILIT means that once it is established and funded, the grantor (the person who sets up the trust) typically cannot alter or dissolve the trust. This strict rule is a key feature that differentiates ILITs from other types of trusts and contributes to their effectiveness in estate planning and asset protection.

The primary purpose of an ILIT is to remove the life insurance policy from the taxable estate of the grantor, ensuring that the death benefit passes to the beneficiaries without being subject to estate taxes. By placing a life insurance policy in an ILIT, the grantor effectively relinquishes ownership of the policy, thereby shielding the death benefit from potential estate tax implications upon their death.

The Structure and Setup of an ILIT

To create an ILIT it is good practice to have a trust document that spells out in detail how the trust is to operate. The trust will typically include who the beneficiaries are, how the trust will operate, identity of the trustee, purpose of the trust, and what assets are involved. Once the ILIT is established, the grantor transfers an existing life insurance policy into the trust or arranges for the trust to purchase a new policy. The trustee's role typically includes paying the life insurance premiums, overseeing the policy, and ensuring compliance with the trust's terms.

The ILIT must be funded to cover premium payments on the insurance policy. This funding can come from annual gifts made by the grantor, which may be subject to annual gift tax exclusions, or if they exceed the annual exclusion amounts may either be taxable, or use up part of the grantor's remaining lifetime exemption. In the latter cases, a gift tax return may be required.

The beneficiaries of the ILIT will typically receive a so-called "Crummey" letter each time a contribution is made to the ILIT. The name "Crummey" is from a 1968 court ruling in a case called Crummey v. Commissioner of Internal Revenue. The Crummey letter typically contains a "Crummey Power", giving each trust beneficiary a temporary right to withdraw the gifted amount, which helps ensure that the gift qualifies for the exclusion.

TRUSTEE

An ILIT must have an independent trustee. The grantor of an ILIT should not serve as the trustee, because doing so would likely bring the assets back into the grantor's estate, defeating the purpose of the ILIT.

To avoid accidentally bringing the trust assets back into the grantor's estate, the grantor must give up control of the life insurance policy and trust assets, and avoid "incidents of ownership."

The trustee should therefore be someone other than the grantor. It's often recommended to name an institutional trustee familiar with ILIT administration, to ensure proper management and compliance with IRS requirements.

Trust Company Recommended

While it seems like it should be a simple matter to be the trustee of an ILIT, potential trustees (particularly potential non-professional trustees who might for example be asked to serve as trustee as a favor) should be aware of potential complications. One such potential complication is unforeseen obligations, such as might arise under the "prudent man rule" or a similar rule in state law.

A 2020 legal case, stemming from a trust created in 1981 (case titled Mfrs. & Traders Trust Co. v. Nielsen (In re Wilkinson), 179 A.D.3d 817, 117 N.Y.S.3d 683 (N.Y. App. Div. 2020), highlights some of the hidden risks.

Beneficiaries of the life insurance policies were supposed to pay the premiums, but did not. Despite an agreement holding the trustee harmless, the trustee was ultimately held liable for making good the death benefit on the lapsed policies, which in aggregate had death benefits over $500,000. Ouch.

THE STRATEGIC USES OF ILITS

Save or Eliminate Estate Taxes

The most prominent use of an ILIT is to reduce or eliminate estate taxes on the life insurance proceeds. Without an ILIT, if the grantor owned the policy, the death benefit would be included in the grantor's gross estate and potentially subject to estate taxes. By transferring life insurance policy ownership to an ILIT, high net worth individuals can ensure that the death benefit passes to beneficiaries without being subject to estate tax, maximizing the value of the legacy to the beneficiaries of the ILIT.

Asset Protection

If an ILIT is drafted with asset protection in mind, the assets it holds are shielded from creditors and potential legal claims against the grantor. This feature helps make ILITs a popular choice for individuals who want to protect their assets from unforeseen liability, business risks, or lawsuits. The death benefit remains secure within the trust, providing financial security for the beneficiaries even if the grantor's personal estate faces claims.

Wealth Transfer and Legacy Planning

ILITs are an effective tool for strategic wealth transfer. By ensuring that the life insurance payout is not subject to estate taxes, the full death benefit can be used to support future generations, used to help offset estate taxes that remain, generate income, and or establish the basis for a dynasty or generation skipping trust.

ILITs can be customized to distribute proceeds over time or in specific amounts, ensuring that beneficiaries are provided for according to the grantor's wishes.

Business Succession Planning

For business owners, ILITs can play a crucial role in succession planning. Life insurance proceeds managed by the trust can provide liquidity to buy out business partners or cover estate taxes, preventing the forced sale of business assets to meet financial obligations. This enables a smoother transition of ownership and sustains the operation of the business after the grantor's death.

Equalizing Inheritances

ILITs can be used as a tool for balancing inheritances among heirs. For example, if one child is more involved in the family business and stands to inherit the business, the life insurance proceeds from an ILIT can be allocated to other children, ensuring a fair distribution of wealth without having to divide business assets.

OTHER CONSIDERATIONS

While ILITs offer numerous benefits, they also come with certain limitations and challenges. Once an ILIT is established and funded, the grantor loses legal control over the assets. This loss of control means that decisions regarding the life insurance policy and the use of trust assets are legally in the hands of the trustee, according to the terms outlined in the trust document. In a well planned and executed situation, these limitations should not create issues.

CONCLUSION

An ILIT is a powerful estate planning tool that can offer substantial tax benefits, asset protection, and strategic wealth transfer opportunities. By understanding how an ILIT functions and incorporating it into a comprehensive estate plan, high net worth individuals can enhance their legacy planning, protect their assets, and provide lasting financial security for their beneficiaries. Properly managed, an ILIT helps ensure that life insurance proceeds fulfill their potential, free from the burdens of estate taxes and liability risks.

Glossary of Initialisms and Acronyms with Explanations

AFR: Applicable Federal Rate
Explanation: The Applicable Federal Rate (AFR) is the minimum interest rate that the IRS allows for private loans, including intra-family loans and certain trust-related transactions.

AGI: Adjusted Gross Income
Explanation: Adjusted Gross Income (AGI) is an individual's total gross income minus specific deductions, used to determine taxable income.

BATF: Bureau of Alcohol, Tobacco and Firearms
Explanation: The Bureau of Alcohol, Tobacco, Firearms and Explosives (BATF) is a federal agency responsible for regulating and investigating federal offenses involving those substances.

CLAT: Charitable Lead Annuity Trust
Explanation: A Charitable Lead Annuity Trust (CLAT) is a type of irrevocable trust that makes annual payments to a charity for a set term, with remaining assets going to non-charitable beneficiaries.

DAPT: Domestic Asset Protection Trust
Explanation: A Domestic Asset Protection Trust (DAPT) is a domestic self-settled trust that allows the grantor to be a beneficiary while protecting the assets from creditors.

DNI: Distributable Net Income
Explanation: Distributable Net Income (DNI) determines how income from a trust is taxed between the trust and its beneficiaries.

ETH: Ethereum
Explanation: Ethereum is a decentralized, open-source blockchain featuring smart contract functionality and the cryptocurrency Ether.

FATCA: Foreign Account Tax Compliance Act
Explanation: The Foreign Account Tax Compliance Act is a U.S. law requiring foreign financial institutions to report assets held by U.S. citizens.

FMV: Fair Market Value
Explanation: Fair Market Value is the price that property would sell for on the open market under normal conditions.

GRAT: Grantor Retained Annuity Trust
Explanation: A Grantor Retained Annuity Trust is an estate planning tool in which the grantor transfers assets while retaining an annuity.

GST: Generation Skipping Tax, or Generation Skipping Trust
Explanation: The Generation-Skipping Tax is a federal tax on transfers of assets to individuals more than one generation below the donor, such as grandchildren. A Generation Skipping Trust is a trust to which generation-skipping exemption has been applied.

IDGT: Intentionally Defective Grantor Trust
Explanation: An Intentionally Defective Grantor Trust is a trust that is ignored for income tax purposes but out of the grantor's estate for estate tax purposes.

ILIT: Irrevocable Life Insurance Trust
Explanation: An Irrevocable Life Insurance Trust is used to hold life insurance policies outside of a taxable estate, preserving death benefits from estate taxation.

IRC: Internal Revenue Code
Explanation: The Internal Revenue Code is the comprehensive body of federal tax law used in the United States.

IRS: Internal Revenue Service
Explanation: The Internal Revenue Service is the U.S. government agency responsible for tax collection and enforcement.

MPT: Modern Portfolio Theory
Explanation: Modern Portfolio Theory is an investment theory that assumes markets are efficient and investors are focused on maximizing return for a given level of risk.

NCREIF: National Council of Real Estate Investment Fiduciaries
Explanation: The National Council of Real Estate Investment Fiduciaries provides performance data and benchmarks for institutional real estate investment.

NIIT: Net Investment Income Tax (also called "NII")
Explanation: The Net Investment Income Tax is a 3.8% surtax on investment income above certain thresholds.

QCD: Qualified Charitable Distribution
Explanation: A Qualified Charitable Distribution allows IRA owners over age 70½ to donate up to $100,000 annually directly to a charity without increasing taxable income.

QPRT: Qualified Personal Residence Trust
Explanation: A Qualified Personal Residence Trust is a type of trust that allows a person to transfer a home at a discounted gift tax value while continuing to live in it for a term.

QTIP: Qualified Terminable Interest Property
Explanation: Qualified Terminable Interest Property trusts allow a surviving spouse to receive income from assets while preserving the principal for other beneficiaries.

SLAT: Spousal Lifetime Access Trust
Explanation: A Spousal Lifetime Access Trust is an irrevocable trust in which one spouse gifts assets while allowing the other spouse to access income or principal.

SNT: Special Needs Trusts
Explanation: A Special Needs Trust holds assets for a disabled beneficiary without affecting their eligibility for government benefits.

SSI: Supplemental Security Income
Explanation: Supplemental Security Income is a federal income supplement program for aged, blind, or disabled people with little or no income.

TAI: Trust Accounting Income

Explanation: Trust Accounting Income is the income determined under the terms of the trust and state law that is available for distribution to income beneficiaries.

UNI: Undistributed Net Income
Explanation: Undistributed Net Income refers to trust income accumulated and not distributed to beneficiaries in prior years.

UTC: Uniform Trust Code
Explanation: The Uniform Trust Code is a standardized set of trust laws designed to harmonize trust regulation across U.S. states.